Foreword

In the thick of battle, the soldier is busy doing his job. He has the knowledge and confidence that his job is part of a unified plan to defeat the enemy, but he does not have time to survey a campaign from a fox hole. If he should be wounded and removed behind the lines, he may have even less opportunity to learn what place he and his unit had in the larger fight.

American forces in action is a series prepared by the War Department especially for the information of wounded men. It will show these soldiers, who have served their country so well, the part they and their comrades played in achievments which do honor to the record of the United States Army.

G. C. MARSHALL,
Chief of Staff.

WAR DEPARTMENT
MILITARY INTELLIGENCE DIVISION
Washington 25, D. C.
1 May 1944

Papuan Campaign, The Buna-Sanananda Operation is the second of a series called AMERICAN FORCES IN ACTION. The series is designed exclusively for military personnel and primarily for wounded in hospitals. It aims to tell them the military story of the campaigns and battles in which they served. No part of this pamphlet may be republished without the consent of the A. C. of S., G–2, War Department, Washington 25, D. C.

This pamphlet is based on the best military records now available. Most of the maps were prepared by the Cartographic Section, Dissemination Unit, M. I. D. Aerial photographs are by the Allied Air Forces, S. W. P. A.; all others, except one from *Life* magazine, are by the U. S. Army Signal Corps. Readers are urged to send directly to the Historical Branch, G–2, War Department, Washington 25, D. C., comments, criticisms, and additional information which may be of value in the preparation of a complete and definitive history of the Buna-Sanananda operation.

PAPUAN CAMPAIGN

The Buna-Sanananda Operation

16 NOVEMBER 1942–23 JANUARY 1943

American Forces in Action Series

MILITARY INTELLIGENCE DIVISION

U.S WAR DEPARTMENT   WASHINGTON, D. C.

Published by Books Express Publishing
Copyright © Books Express, 2011
ISBN 978-1-78039-083-3

Books Express publications are available from all good retail and online booksellers. For
publishing proposals and direct ordering please contact us at: info@books-express.com

Table of Contents

INTRODUCTION

PART I—BUNA

PART II—SANANANDA

Maps

Sketches

Photographs

INTRODUCTION
The Japanese Threat to Australia

(Map No. 1, inside back cover)

DURING the early months of 1942 the Japanese were on the offensive everywhere in the Southwest Pacific and their armies seemed to be invincible. On 10 December 1941, Japanese forces landed in the Philippines; on 15 February 1942, Singapore fell; within a month the Netherlands Indies were conquered. Then the attack shifted farther to the southeast, and from Rabaul in New Britain, which had been occupied on 23 January, the Japanese High Command planned a two-pronged drive. One prong was to strike for control of southeastern New Guinea; the other was to thrust through the Solomon Islands to cut the supply line from America to Australia.

Neither attack reached its objective. When a Japanese convoy pushed around the eastern tip of New Guinea threatening Port Moresby and northeastern Australia, it met American naval forces. In the ensuing Battle of the Coral Sea (4–8 May 1942), the Japanese suffered a decisive defeat. Five months later, the Japanese advance toward our supply line in the Southwest Pacific ended when American marines landed (7 August) in the Solomons on Tulagi, Gavutu, Florida, and Guadalcanal.

Failure in their attempt by sea did not end the Japanese effort to capture Port Moresby, which would afford them an invasion base only 340 miles from the Cape York Peninsula in Australia. In July they landed at Buna, Gona, and Sanananda on the northeast coast of Papua and pushed southward across the Papuan Peninsula. The Australians first stopped the enemy and then, joined by American forces, drove him back to his landing bases . The Allied campaign culminated in the capture of those bases. This long and hard counteroffensive not only freed Australia from the imminent threat of invasion, but gave the United Nations their first toehold in the area of enemy defenses protecting Rabaul, center of Japanese power in the Southwest Pacific.

The American part in the Buna-Sanananda campaign, in which Australian and American troops defeated "the invincible Imperial Army" of Japan, is the subject of this pamphlet. The proportion of American troops in the Allied forces at Buna was much greater than at Sanananda, and for this reason the Buna operation receives the more detailed treatment. The story is set in a background of fever-ridden swamp and jungle, where American soldiers lay day after day in waterlogged fox holes or crawled through murderous fire toward enemy positions they could not see. Despite all the difficulties imposed by terrain, climate, and the formidable strength of Japanese fortifications, despite failure in many heroic attacks, the effort was carried through to a final and smashing success. This campaign and the almost simultaneous action on Guadalcanal were the first victorious operations of U. S. ground forces against the Japanese.

Beginning of the Allied Counteroffensive
(*Map No. 2, page 3*)

On 21 and 22 July a Japanese convoy of 3 transports, 2 light cruisers, and 3 destroyers reached Gona and disembarked Maj. Gen. Tomitaro Horii with about 4,400 troops. Allied Air Force attacks succeeded in setting fire to 1 transport. Additional troops and supplies poured in during the next few days. By 13 August 11,100 men had landed and the drive on Port Moresby began. The Japanese fought their way across the deep gorges and razor-backed ridges of the Owen Stanley Mountains and descended the southern slopes to within 32 miles of the port. Here Australian resistance stiffened and on 14 September the advance was held at Imita Range, south of Ioribaiwa.

During the next 2 weeks the Allied Air Force continued relentless strafing and bombing of the Japanese supply lines running over the mountains to Buna, Sanananda, and Gona. The enemy, half-starved, attacked on front and flank by the Australians, yielded Ioribaiwa on 28 September and began to withdraw hastily up the trail. During the critical last days of August, Japanese units had landed at Milne Bay

SOUTH—EAST
NEW GUINEA
(PAPUAN PENINSULA)

SCALE

MILES

Cartographic Section, Dir's LHd by J.R. Hogan

3

to threaten Port Moresby from the east, but this attack had been quickly stopped. After 3 days of heavy fighting, the enemy troops were forced back to the beach and taken off by naval vessels. For the first time, a Japanese force had been evacuated after failing in its mission.

Just as the tide of invasion began to ebb, American troops entered the New Guinea theater of operations. Early in September, when the Japanese threat appeared most grave, the 126th Infantry Combat Team and the 128th Infantry Combat Team, both of the 32d Division, were ordered to Port Moresby from Australia. Each combat team was composed of a regiment of infantry, a platoon of the 114th Engineers, a Collecting Company and a platoon of the Clearing Company of the 107th Medical Battalion with three 25-bed portable hospitals, and a detachment of the 32d Signal Company. The infantry howitzers, divisional artillery, and about two-thirds of the 81-mm mortars were left behind because of the difficulties of transportation to the Buna area.

The 32d Division was a National Guard unit from Michigan and Wisconsin, commanded at this time by Maj. Gen. Edwin F. Harding. It had been sent to Australia in April 1942 and had there received a very brief and sketchy training in jungle warfare. Though the Buna-Sanananda campaign was its first combat experience in World War II, the division could look back on an excellent record in World War I, when it had been one of the first units to reach France.

The transfer of the two combat teams to Port Moresby, partly by plane and partly by boat, was completed on 28 September. The 128th Infantry occupied positions on the Allied left flank to operate up the Goldie River. The 126th Infantry went into bivouac near Port Moresby, while a patrol, under the command of Capt. William F. Boice, proceeded east along the coast to look for a route over the mountains on the Allied right flank.[1]

Allied strategy in New Guinea now began to shift from defense to counterattack. The Japanese, closely pursued by the Australians, continued their rapid retreat toward Kokoda. Intelligence reports indi-

---

[1] The 127th Infantry Combat Team disembarked at Port Moresby almost 2 months later, on Thanksgiving Day. On 27 December, the 163d Infantry reached New Guinea from Australia. This unit of the 41st Division was also a National Guard Regiment sent to Australia in April 1942.

4

cated that no enemy reinforcements were reaching the Buna-Sanan-anda area. The enemy was apparently concentrating all his available naval, air, and land strength on the battle then raging in the Solomons. If he could drive us from Guadalcanal and advance southward to cut our supply line to Australia, his relative neglect of New Guinea would be justified. On the other hand, determined action on our part might crush the enemy in the Papuan Peninsula and so remove permanently the Japanese threat to Port Moresby.

General Douglas MacArthur, Commander-in-Chief, Southwest Pacific Area; General Sir Thomas Blamey, Commander of Allied Land Forces, Southwest Pacific Area and General Officer Commanding New Guinea Force; and Lt. Gen. E. F. Herring, General Officer Commanding Advanced New Guinea Force, all of whom were at Port Moresby, laid their plans accordingly. While the Australians continued to drive the enemy back along the Kokoda trail, the 32d Division under General Harding would make a secret, wide envelopment to the east and attack in force on the enemy left flank in the vicinity of Buna. This move might cut off the retreat of the main Japanese force facing the Australians. To insure speed and to avoid dissipating the strength of the division by marching it across the exhausting mountain trails, most of the enveloping force was to go by air to the seacoast southeast of Buna.

During the remainder of October and the early part of November, the 126th Infantry and the 128th Infantry were moving into position. Acting as left-flank guard, the 2d Battalion of the 126th Infantry crossed the lofty Owen Stanley Mountains on foot by a rugged trail rising over 8,000 feet. On 20 November, after an exceedingly difficult march of 5 weeks, they reached Soputa. The 128th Infantry on 14–18 October was flown to the hastily improved air strip at Wanigela Mission on Collinwood Bay, 65 air miles from Buna. From Wanigela small 20-ton motor launches carried the regiment up the coast to Pongani, 23 miles from Buna, where it halted to construct a landing strip. The 126th Infantry, less the 2d Battalion and part of the 1st Battalion, went directly by air to this new strip on 9–11 November.

While our troops were concentrating toward Buna, reconnaissance was limited in order to secure the maximum of surprise when the force attacked. However, Australian patrols operating to our front learned early in November that "bush wireless" had carried the news of our

Organization of the Allied Forces in New Guinea (16 November 1942–23 January 1943)

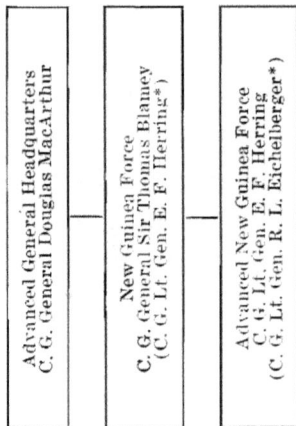

```
                    Advanced General Headquarters
                    C. G. General Douglas MacArthur

                              |

                         New Guinea Force
                    C. G. General Sir Thomas Blamey
                    (C. G. Lt. Gen. E. F. Herring*)

                              |

                    Advanced New Guinea Force
                    C. G. Lt. Gen. E. F. Herring
                    (C. G. Lt. Gen. R. L. Eichelberger*)
```

AUSTRALIAN UNITS

Headquarters, Aust. 7th Division
    C. G. Maj. Gen. G. A. Vasey
Aust. 2/7 Cavalry Regiment
Aust. 2/6 Armored Regiment

Infantry
Aust. 14th Infantry Brigade (Attached)
Aust. 16th Infantry Brigade (Attached)
Aust. 18th Infantry Brigade
Aust. 21st Infantry Brigade
Aust. 25th Infantry Brigade
Aust. 30th Infantry Brigade (Attached)
Aust. 2/6 Independent Company

Artillery
One battery, Aust. 2/1 Field Regiment (Attached)
One troop, Aust. 2/5 Field Regiment
One troop, Aust. 13th Field Regiment (Attached)
Aust. 1st Mountain Battery (Attached)

U. S. UNITS

Headquarters, U. S. I Corps
    C. G. Lt. Gen. R. L. Eichelberger

Infantry
32d Division
    126th Infantry Regimental Combat Team
    127th Infantry Regimental Combat Team
    128th Infantry Regimental Combat Team
41st Division
    163d Infantry Regimental Combat Team

*After the fall of Buna Mission General MacArthur and General Blamey returned to their headquarters in Australia. Then General Herring commanded the New Guinea Force and General Eichelberger commanded the Advanced New Guinea Force.

approach to the enemy, and therefore from 10 November the troops advanced as rapidly as possible.

By the evening of 18 November the forward movement had brought our forces close to Buna (Map No. 3, facing page 9). The 1st Battalion, 128th Infantry, was on the coastal track between Hariko and the Duropa Plantation; the 1st Battalion, 126 Infantry, was coming up from Oro Bay along the same trail . The bulk of the 126th Infantry was in position on the left in the vicinity of Inonda. Beyond was the Australian 7th Division pushing forward on the trails to Gona and Sanananda. The 3d Battalion of the 128th was near Simemi; the 2d Battalion, in division reserve, was split between Ango and the grassy plain at Dobodura. Here E Company and the Cannon Company were working at top speed with a detachment of the 114th Engineers to construct a landing strip needed for transport planes and fighters. Speed was vital if the division was to eat, for on 16-17 November two enemy air attacks on our small boats had crippled the coastal line of supply.

Enemy patrolling to our front had increased during the past few days, but despite this activity, the garrison in Buna appeared to be very weak. Native reports indicated that the Japanese had retreated to the landing strips at Buna. The men of the 32d Division expected to end the campaign with one quick attack and advanced full of enthusiasm. A month later, still facing Buna, our troops would look back with envy on the relatively easy days of the approach march, when they had slogged along muddy trails and waded breast-high streams.

On the Way to Buna: The Inland Route.

Men of M Company, 128th Infantry, on the trail between Dobodura and Buna.

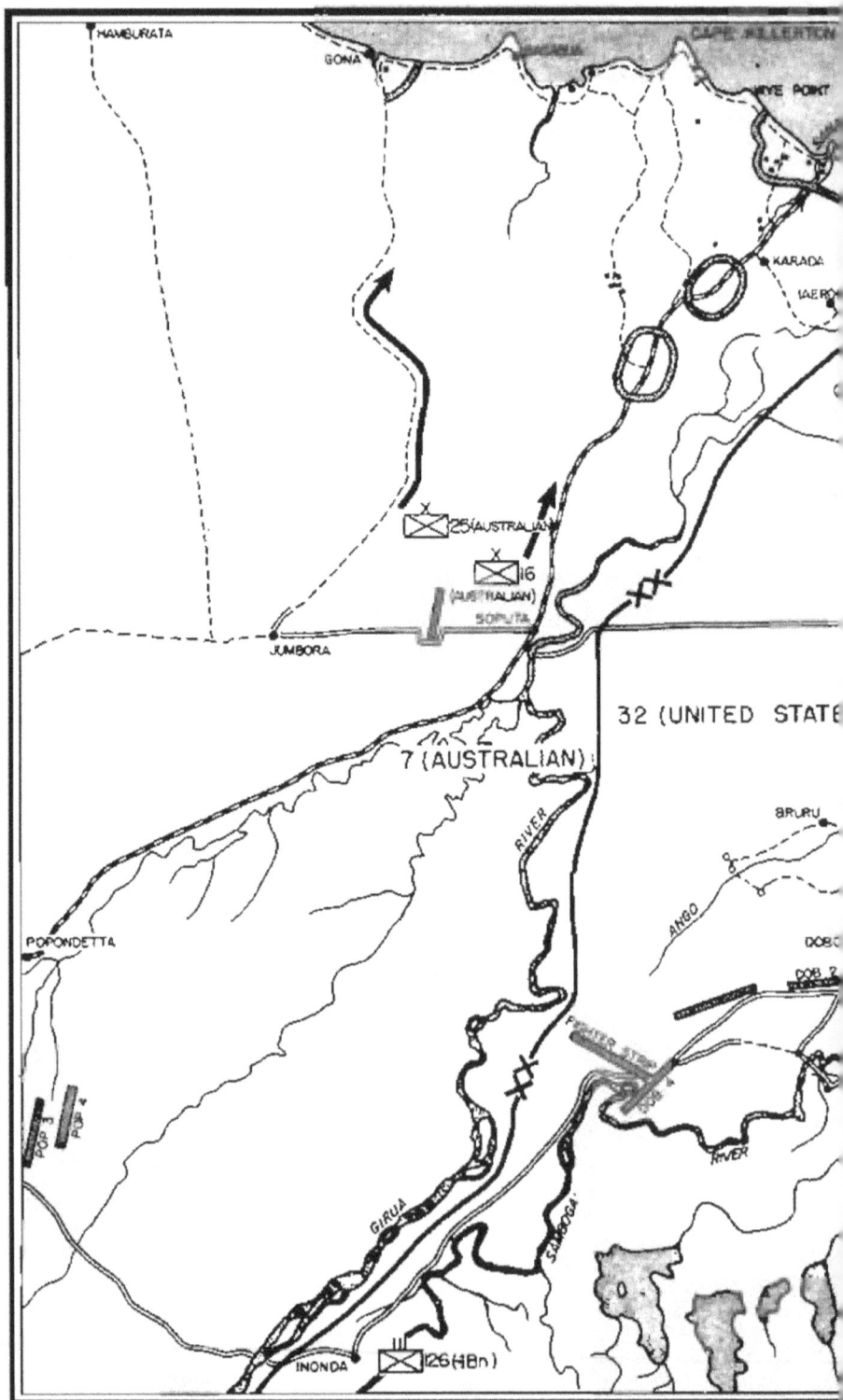

THAMBURATA · GONA · CAPE KILLERTON · WYE POINT · KARADA · IAERO

25 (AUSTRALIAN)

116 (AUSTRALIAN)

SOPUTA

JUMBORA

7 (AUSTRALIAN)

32 (UNITED STATE

BRURU

ANGO

DOBC

DOB. 2

POPONDETTA

POP 3 · POP 4

FISTER STRIP

GIRUA RIVER

RIVER

SAMBOGA RIVER

INONDA · 126 (Bn)

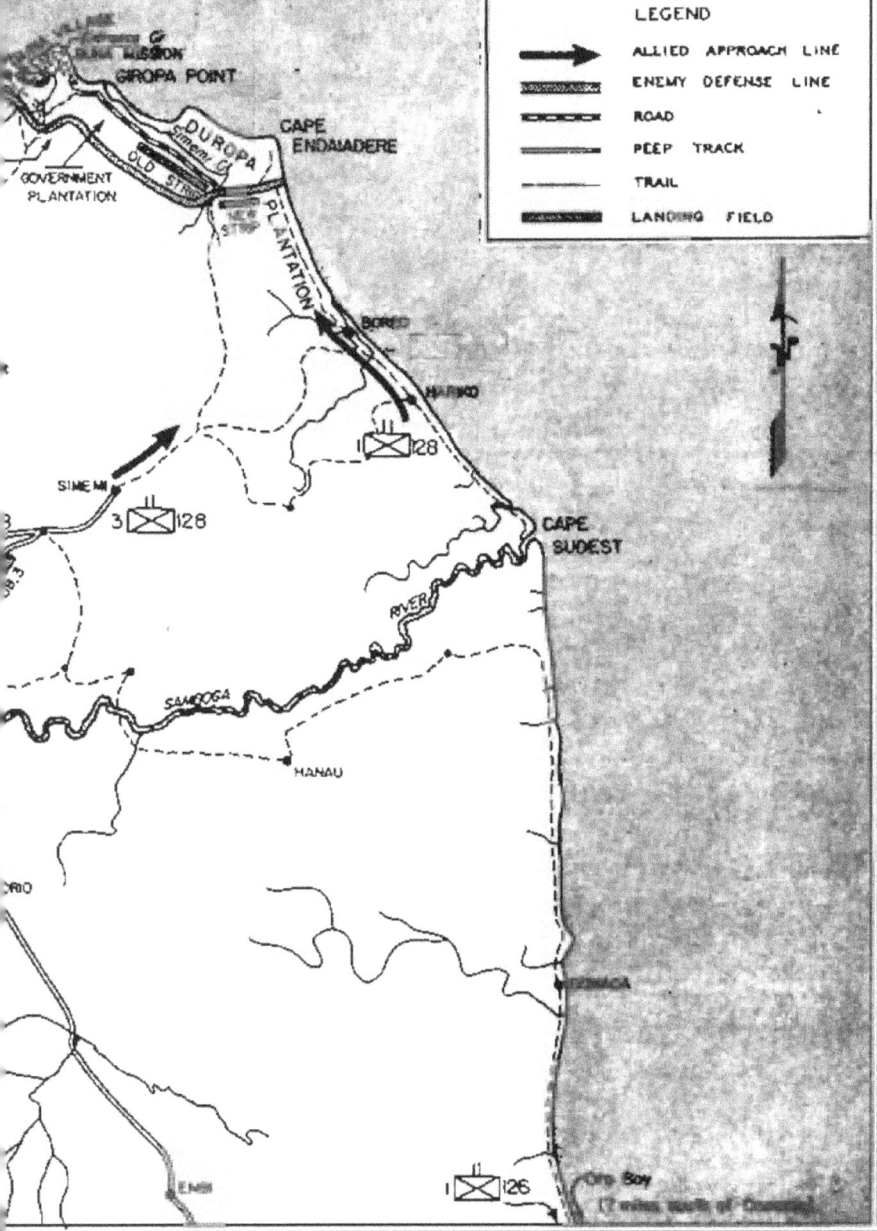

BUNA — SANANANDA

SITUATION 18 NOVEMBER 1942

SCALE

MILES

LEGEND

ALLIED APPROACH LINE
ENEMY DEFENSE LINE
ROAD
PEEP TRACK
TRAIL
LANDING FIELD

PART I—BUNA

Background of the Buna Operation

THE ENEMY had taken cunning advantage of the peculiar geography of the Buna area to construct two almost impregnable defensive lines hidden in the swampy jungle. One of these lay across the Soputa-Sanananda Road; the other was in front of Buna itself. Our forces on 18 November had only the vaguest notion of these fortifications. The campaign cannot be understood without a description of the area, of its climate, and of the Japanese defenses.

The fighting took place in a narrow strip on the northeastern coast of Papua extending on both sides of Buna Mission, the prewar seat of government for the area. The Mission, sometimes called the Government Station, consisted of three houses and a few dozen native huts. Buna Village, a half mile to the northwest, was merely a cluster of huts. Bounded on the west by one of the several outlets of the Girua River and on the east by the coast a half mile south of Cape Endaiadere, the battleground was about 3½ miles long and ¾ of a mile deep. To a casual observer, the area would seem to be merely typical Papuan terrain, with its irregular pattern of steaming jungle, impassable swamp, coconut plantations, and open fields of coarse, shoulder-high kunai grass. Our troops came to know and to distinguish the smallest terrain features, usually the result of differences in vegetation.

Variations in the elevation played little part in the Buna landscape for the whole area is a flat, low-lying plain. The landing field at Buna is 5 feet above sea level, and even at Soputa, 7½ miles inland, the land rises only to an elevation of 10 feet. The sluggish rivers that run north from the Owen Stanley Mountains lose themselves in swamps of nipa, mangrove, and sago trees, which often extend to the coast. The Girua River is typical. It is 40 to 60 feet wide until it disappears in the swamps southeast of Buna Village, and it eventually reaches the ocean through several mouths between Buna and Sanananda. One of these mouths is Entrance Creek, which opens into a shallow lagoon between Buna Village and Buna Mission. Simemi Creek, another stream important in the fighting, runs north to the vicinity of the Buna airfield and then parallels the northern edge of the field to the sea.

The principal swamp in the Buna area lies between Entrance Creek and Simemi Creek and reaches inland to the vicinity of Simemi and Ango. It is absolutely impenetrable, a fact of vital importance in the campaign. Between the closely spaced trees, which are 25 to 100 feet high, is a tangle of roots, creepers, and underbrush. A man standing up can see from 5 to 30 yards; from a fox hole visibility is practically zero. Much of the other ground in the area, though not actually swamp, is thoroughly waterlogged, but a few places near the shore are fairly dry.

Most of the drier land is covered with a thick growth of kunai grass or plantations of coconut palms. This coarse grass grows to a height of more than 6 feet, but its height varies greatly, depending on how recently it has been burned over or cut. Its leaves are broad and sharp-edged; its stems are about the thickness of a pencil. The coconut palms are usually planted about 18 feet apart and the ground under them is relatively clear of cover. Between the mouth of Simemi Creek and Buna Mission lies a government coconut plantation about 300 yards wide; running south from Cape Endaiadere is the Duropa Plantation, about 700 yards wide and 1,800 yards long. To the southwest of this latter plantation is a large area overgrown with kunai grass. Another even larger area of grass occupies the region to the north of the main swamp.

In this open ground southeast of the Mission lies the most important objective of the Allied drive, the landing field. This landing field is 105 air miles from Port Moresby, 147 from Salamaua, and 400 from Rabaul. In Allied hands it would definitely check any enemy threat by land to Port Moresby and, as proved later, would be a powerful support for further advance along the north coast of New Guinea. The landing field was in existence before the Japanese came, but during the enemy occupation it was enlarged to an area 1,300 yards by 90 yards, running southeast and northwest, and dispersal bays were added. Japanese planes used the field until the end of September, when our Air Force pocked its surface with bomb craters and put it out of commission. The Japanese had also built a dummy field, running almost due east and west, in the other grassy area, across Simemi Creek. To distinguish it from the "Old Strip," the dummy field received the name of "New Strip" in our operations.

Approach to Buna is difficult whether by sea or by land. It has no harbor. Coral reefs abound near the shore and are scattered over the sea to a distance of 25 miles from land. Cargo has to be discharged at sea into native double canoes usually carrying 1 to 1½ tons. On the land side, Buna is cut off by swamps and creeks and can be approached only along four narrow corridors, each with its trail.

The coastal trail runs from Cape Sudest past Hariko and cuts over along the northern edge of the New Strip to Simemi Creek, southeast of the Old Strip. Here it meets the second trail, which comes from Dobodura and Simemi village and skirts the east side of the main swamp south of Buna. After the junction, the trail crosses the creek on a permanent bridge and continues along the northern edge of the Old Strip to the Mission. Between the bridge and the Mission, it is a passable motor road. The third trail comes up from Dobodura on the west side of the main swamp, joins a trail from Soputa at Ango Corner, and then runs to a fork about 1,200 yards from the coast. The right fork leads to the coastal track southeast of the Mission; the left fork crosses Entrance Creek by a footbridge and proceeds to Buna Village.

The fourth route approaches Buna from the northwest. It originates beyond Gona and roughly follows the coast, fording several streams before it reaches Siwori Village where it meets two other trails. One of these leads from Siwori Village along the small peninsula between Girua River and the sea to a point just across the mouth of the river from Buna Village. The other skirts the mainland, crosses the Girua River by a footbridge (destroyed early in the operation), and joins the left fork of the Ango trail about 200 yards south of Buna Village. These trails average 12 feet in width but are so low-lying that a heavy rain would put sections under water. The 114th Engineers worked constantly putting down corduroy to make routes passable for peeps, for all supply and evacuation were based on the trails, the "Main Streets" of the Buna jungle.

Along with difficulties resulting from the terrain went problems inherent in the uniformly hot and muggy climate. At Buna a rise in temperature of 1° or 2° F. increases physical discomfort tremendously. To make matters worse, the fighting took place in the months when precipitation, temperature, and humidity are highest. In December of a normal year, the temperature ranges between 72° and 89° F., and the humidity averages 82 per cent. During this month, the average precipitation of 14½ inches falls in heavy tropical showers with intervening periods of clear weather. Fortunately the major rains held off until the very end of the operations at Buna, but the men who fought in the jungle swamps of the northeastern coast of Papua would not describe the area as dry at any time.

Our troops suffered from malaria and dengue fever prevalent in the region. They also suffered from depression and lassitude caused by the climate and inadequate food; salt and vitamin tablets did no more than alleviate the situation. Within 2 weeks of our entry into the area the rate of sickness began to climb, and at all times thereafter a heavy percentage of every combat unit was hospitalized by malaria and other fevers. For every two men who were battle casualties, five were out of action from fever. Daily doses of quinine or atabrine were compulsory but only suppressed the symptoms.

Jungle, swamp, stifling climate, insects, fever—all these and the Japanese were the enemies of our troops. In the words of one of their own number:

The men at the front in New Guinea were perhaps among the most wretched-looking soldiers ever to wear the American uniform. They were gaunt and thin, with deep black circles under their sunken eyes. They were covered with tropical sores. . . . They were clothed in tattered, stained jackets and pants. . . . Often the soles had been sucked off their shoes by the tenacious, stinking mud. Many of them fought for days with fevers and didn't know it. . . . Malaria, dengue fever, dysentery, and, in a few cases, typhus hit man after man. There was hardly a soldier, among the thousands who went into the jungle, who didn't come down with some kind of fever at least once.[2]

---

[2] WO E. J. Kahn, Jr., *G. I. Jungle*, New York; Simon and Schuster, 1943, pp. 121–122.

More than 1,800 seasoned Japanese soldiers and marines, who for the most part had not participated in the Moresby drive, were entrenched in a superb defensive position awaiting our attack. The western flank of the enemy line was protected by the sea and the impenetrable swamps of the main mouth of the Girua River. The eastern flank rested on the seacoast south of Cape Endaiadere. The middle of the line was guarded by the wide stretch of continuous swamp between Entrance and Simemi creeks. Our attacks were necessarily confined to the trails, canalized along two widely separated corridors without any lateral communication, one between Simemi Creek and the east coast and the other on the west side of the swamp along the Ango trail toward the Mission and Buna Village. Movement of our troops from one flank to the other entailed a 2-day march via Ango and Simemi; in contrast, the Japanese had a motor road from the Mission to Simemi Creek over which they could reinforce either flank in a few minutes.

The Japanese main line of defense ran from the Girua River along the outskirts of Buna Village, thence roughly southeast to Entrance Creek and across it to the nearby junction of the Village trail with the Mission-Ango track. There it turned abruptly north, enclosing a narrow pointed area called the Triangle, then swept east across the grass-covered field known as Government Gardens toward Giropa Point. About 500 yards south of the Point it bent southeast to the western end of the Old Strip. This western sector was manned by two Marine units, the Yasuda Butai (detachment) and the Tsukioka Butai, under Col. Yoshitatsu Yasuda. Men of these units had fought in China, Malaya, and various islands of the Pacific.

The south edge of the Old Strip was protected by the swamp. From the bridge across Simemi Creek at the southeastern corner of the Old Strip, the enemy defense line continued along the northern edge of the New Strip through the Duropa Plantation to reach the sea a half mile south of Cape Endaiadere. The 3d Battalion, 229th Infantry,[3] which had fought at Canton and Hongkong, marched down from Gona on 18 November and manned this eastern flank, together with a replacement unit known as the Yamamoto Butai.

---

[3] The 1st and 2d Battalions, 229th Infantry, it may be noted, were at this time on Guadalcanal.

These troops were commanded by Maj. Gen. Oda, succeeding General Horii, who had been drowned in the Kumusi River while retreating from the attack on Port Moresby. In addition to the infantry already mentioned, which numbered about 1,165, he had at Buna a number of other elements: a heavy antiaircraft battery which was tentatively identified as the 73d Independent Unit, with a minimum strength of 100; a battery of mountain artillery believed to be from the 3d Battalion, 55th Field Artillery, and numbering at least 100 men; about 100 men remaining from the 144th Infantry, which had been decimated in the Port Morsby expedition; some 300 miscellaneous troops, including engineer, medical, signal, and supply personnel; about 400 Japanese, Formosan, and Korean laborers of the 14th and 15th Construction Units. The Japanese force at Buna thus totaled about 2,200, of which some 1,800 were combat troops. Only the remnant of the 144th Infantry had taken part in the disastrous retreat over the Owen Stanley Mountains; the rest were fresh and ready for battle.

Our troops approached Buna completely ignorant of the defenses which faced them. They found the enemy forces established in almost impregnable defensive works, which baffled the earlier attackers and left them uncertain of the exact location of their foes. They first had to find out just where the Japanese were and then solve the problem of how to drive them from their fortifications.

The defenses consisted essentially of a network of mutually supporting bunkers, organized in depth. The 32d Division at Buna was the first American unit to meet and conquer this type of defense. At Munda, Salamaua, and all other points in the Southwest Pacific Area where we have since encountered prepared Japanese positions, the experience gained at Buna has proved valuable.

Dugouts are not feasible in the Buna area because the water table is too close to the surface. The Japanese bunkers were, therefore, almost entirely above ground. The base of the bunker was a shallow trench, up to 40 feet in length for the larger bunkers, and 6 to 10 feet for the smaller. A framework of columns and beams was set up, the walls were revetted with coconut logs ranging up to 1½ feet in thickness, and a ceiling of two or three courses of such logs was laid on top. Not content with this construction, the enemy reinforced the wall, using steel oil drums and ammunition boxes filled with sand, as well as log

Japanese Bunker in the Duropa Plantation.
Cpl. Charles Claridge of Reedsburg, Wisconsin, is looking at the entrance.

Interior of a Japanese Bunker in the Duropa Plantation.
Note the sand-filled oil drums used to reinforce the palm-log structure.

15

piles and rocks. Over all this were piled earth and sand mixed with short logs, coconuts, and the like. When the bunker, 7 to 8 feet high, was camouflaged with fast-growing jungle vegetation, it became almost impossible to spot in the tangled underbrush. The campaign was to prove that as a shelter it would withstand almost anything but a direct hit by a heavy artillery shell with delayed-action fuze. Entrances to the bunkers usually were in the rear, covered by fire from adjacent bunkers, and often angled so that a hand grenade tossed in the door would not kill the occupants.

Some of the bunkers had fire slits for machine guns or rifles. In this case snipers in the trees overhead served as observers. The snipers would fire warning shots when our troops approached, and then a machine-gun burst would come from the bunker. The bunkers, however, were principally used for shelter during aerial bombardment and shelling. After such attacks the Japanese crawled out along the communication trenches and took up firing positions in individual emplacements to the sides and front of the bunkers. Not all of these shelters were occupied at any one time; the garrison shifted from point to point to meet our attack, and our troops soon learned that each captured bunker must be garrisoned or destroyed to prevent the enemy from infiltrating and reoccupying it. The Japanese worked steadily to improve and strengthen their system of defenses and constructed new lines as they were forced back.

Japanese tactics during the Buna campaign were strictly defensive. Counterattacks were few and came mostly at the end of the operation, when the enemy's situation was growing desperate. For the most part he dug himself in and waited for our troops to cross his final protective lines. Time and time again our troops were baffled by the enfilading fire from positions they could not see. As the soldiers kept complaining, "If we could only see them, it wouldn't take long." But the Japanese light machine guns and Arisaka rifles gave off no flash, and in the great tent of towering trees sound so reverberated that the report of a weapon did not aid in its location. Our troops had to locate each bunker by costly fumbling, then either outflank it by creeping through a swamp or charge it again and again until the defenders were worn out. The Japanese never surrendered. As one soldier explained, "They are tough babies all right, but I guess part of the toughness comes from them not being able to go any place else; they just stay there and die."

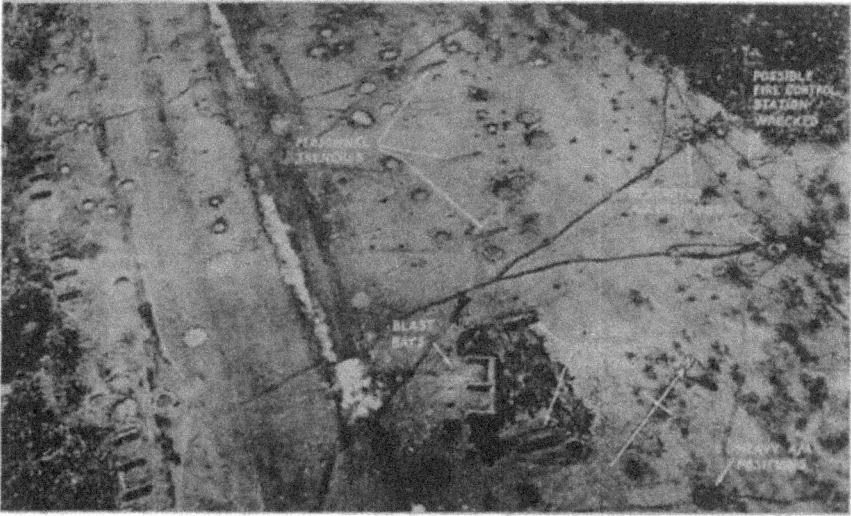

The Old Strip, Buna, Showing Japanese Fortifications.

Firing Pits and Bunker Entrances, Buna Mission.

Our victory at Buna was the fruit of cooperation between ground
and air forces. Either without the other would have failed. The Australian and American units of the U. S. 5th Air Force, under Lt. Gen.
George C. Kenney, met all demands, strategic, tactical, and logistic.
Though our squadrons were often outnumbered and always short of
pilots, planes, and supplies, they were stronger than the forces which
the Japanese could spare from their major effort in the Solomons. The
skill and courage of Allied fliers, in combination with the superiority
of our planes, won aerial mastery over the southeastern end of New
Guinea. Our control of the air made large-scale reinforcement of the
enemy troops in the area cost more than the Japanese were willing or
able to pay in terms of losses. At the same time, we were able to bring
in the soldiers and supplies to drive the enemy from Buna and
Sanananda.

Our control of the air was won by constant patrolling, armed reconnaissance, and aggressive fighter operations.[4] Yet we could not
monopolize the air and considerable numbers of hostile planes from
time to time succeeded in breaking through to bomb and strafe our
troops and rear areas. For example, on 7 December, 3 Japanese navy
dive bombers and 18 Zero-escorted high-level bombers attacked the 2d
Field Hospital at Simemi, causing heavy casualties. As late as 27
December, when the enemy was withdrawing toward the sea for his
last stand, 41 Zeros and dive bombers attempted to raid our positions
but were intercepted by 8 of our P-38's. Two enemy planes were shot
down, and the 3 bombs dropped did no damage. However, the

[4] Tabulation of cooperation by the 5th Air Force in the New Guinea area, 1 November 1942–
23 January 1943:

NUMBER OF MISSIONS ASSIGNED

Type of plane	Aerial recon- naissance and observation	Armed recon- naissance, escort, and patrol	Attack on enemy aircraft	Bombing and strafing	Total
Heavy Bomber		116	1	47	164
Medium Bomber		45		88	133
Light Bomber		28		74	102
Fighter	35	38	3	63	139
Miscellaneous		73			73
Total	35	300	4	272	611

enemy could not maintain a continuous or effective aerial offensive and suffered severe losses in his occasional raids. He never completely severed our fragile lines of communication.

Strategic bombing and strafing of enemy airfields at Lae, Salamaua, and Rabaul by the 5th Air Force was severely limited by the small number of planes available. Between 1 November 1942 and 31 January 1943, only 13½ tons of explosives were dropped on ground targets and shipping outside the coastal region of southeastern New Guinea. At the same time, however, the 13th Air Force was engaging large numbers of Japanese planes in the Solomons and was also bombing Rabaul. These attacks had an effect out of proportion to their apparent weight, for they compelled the enemy to allocate part of his strength to defense of his bases and restricted his ability to interfere with Allied operations in the Buna-Sanananda area.

Tactical bombing and strafing of enemy forward areas played a relatively small part, for such operations early proved almost as dangerous to our own troops as to the enemy. Contact between our ground units and those of the enemy was exceedingly close and aerial observation was practically impossible. Enemy rear areas were constantly pounded by our B–25's and A–20's, yet during the 6 weeks of active operations only 163 tons of bombs were dropped and 144,790 rounds of ammunition fired on the Buna Mission and Old Strip area. Bombardiers in the combat zone usually had to aim at jungle-covered ground targets visible only at extremely low altitudes. In most instances, pilots had to report "results unobserved." Nevertheless, these raids had telling effect on Japanese forward supply lines and Japanese morale.

Tactical aerial reconnaissance and observation were likewise very difficult, but proved invaluable to our ground forces. A flight of Australian Wirraways, based at Dobodura late in November, gathered information contributing to a precision in artillery fire otherwise impossible because of the inaccuracy of available maps.

Transport, Supply, and Communication

Of first importance and most novel was the contribution of the 5th Air Force to the transport and supply of the ground troops. Most of our infantrymen and supporting troops, a total of 14,900 were flown to the Buna area in the uncomfortable bucket seats of C–47's. The small amount of artillery used in the operation was all airborne for at least part of the way. The air movement of the 128th Infantry from Australia to New Guinea was the first large-scale airborne troop movement by United States forces in a theater of operations. The bulk of the other units of the Buna Force, including the 127th and 163d Infantry Regiments, were flown by the 374th Troop Carrier Group directly to Dobodura and Popondetta, only 10 miles from the front lines. When they were wounded or when they fell ill of tropical diseases, the troops left as they had come; the planes which brought in reinforcements and supplies returned to Port Moresby laden with hospital cases, many of which were ferried immediately by air to Australia.

Supply of rations and equipment was an extraordinarily difficult problem throughout the operation. Land transportation across the mountains was almost impossible and very impractical, since there was only a rough and steep foot trail from Port Moresby to the front and a trip over this trail took 18 to 28 days. The distance could be flown by plane in 35 minutes. While units near the coast relied on supply by small boats, those inland had to depend on supply by aircraft.

The Air Force maintained a regular shuttle service across the treacherous mountains and over the coastal jungle to deliver food for the soldiers and native carriers, as well as the ammunition, the ¼-ton peeps used for transport on the corduroy trails, pick mattocks, shovels, axes, oil for the ordnance which was corroding in the steaming jungle, cots, blankets, surgical instruments, dressings, plasma, quinine and atabrine tablets for the sick and wounded, new shoes, and clothing. The only 105-mm howitzer used in the campaign was carried to the front by aircraft. Sixteen C–47's and several A–29's, based at Ward's Drome, Port Moresby, delivered a total of 2,450 tons to the landing strips at Dobodura, Popondetta, and Pongani and dropped 166 tons at small grounds designated along the jungle trails. Small arms, ammunition, mortar shells, and medical supplies were dropped with parachutes; food, clothing, and individual equipment other than arms, without parachutes.

The losses in dropping without parachutes averaged 50 per cent. For example, cans of bully beef broke open and spoiled. Dropping grounds were hard to find; smudge fires and panels often did not

Strip No. 4 at Dobodura.

American Troops Embarking in a C–47.

identify the area sufficiently, and occasionally loads landed in enemy territory. Hungry men watched every incoming plane for good drops. "Convey our compliments to pilot and crew of *Dutch Boy.* They really laid delivery on the door step," said Maj. Herbert M. Smith, speaking for the 2d Battalion, 126th Infantry.

Pilots made their turn-around as quickly as possible. Two planes, *Sleepy Sally* and *Eager Beaver,* on 4 December made two trips from Port Moresby to Hariko, a distance of 90 miles, and dropped both loads at Hariko within 2 hours and 15 minutes.

Approximately half of the supplies were seaborne. On 14 November, 45 tons a week of rations for the men on the east flank were ordered shipped to Pongani via Milne Bay. Cargoes were transferred at Milne Bay from ocean freighters to smaller vessels of 50 to 500 tons, which crept around East Cape and through Ward Hunt Strait to Oro Bay. Enemy planes and surface craft made it dangerous for ships to remain at Oro Bay during daylight hours, so loads were transferred to smaller craft which made hazardous nightly runs through reef-studded coastal waters to an advance supply base. There the troops, partly infantry, partly units of the 107th Quartermaster Battalion, put out through the surf in native outrigger canoes and unloaded the cases of food and equipment.

This seaborne supply line remained always under threat of interruption. Attacks by enemy planes on 16–17 November put it out of operation for 3 weeks. The 22d Portable Hospital on the *Alacrity,* one of the four boats sunk in the first of these attacks, lost four men and all of its equipment and supplies. On 23 December, two enemy PT-type boats sank a ship off Hariko and machine-gunned the supply base. However, through most of the period, the Allied forces on the east flank were successfully supplied by the sea route.

The chain of supply stretched 1,700 miles from bases in Australia to the landing fields, dropping grounds, and coastal dumps. From such forward points, cargoes had to be transported to the men in and directly behind the combat lines. This last vital transport link was formed by a few peeps and some 700 fuzzy-headed native carriers, who delivered their 40 pounds apiece to dumps just outside the range of small-arms fire.

Requests for supplies flowed from the front to Lt. Col. Ralph T. Birkeness, Division Quartermaster at Port Moresby. All were marked

Native Stretcher Bearers with Wounded American.
On the trail from the Buna Front to Simemi.

Supplies for Headquarters.
Native carriers and guards on the trail from Oro Bay to the Buna Front.

urgent. He had to assign priorities on the limited space of the planes and boats, determining whether the soldiers would receive bullets or rations, or food for the natives who were indispensable as carriers and would go home unless fed, or replacements for the ordnance watches "going to hell" in the damp climate of the Papuan jungle and needed for synchronization of combat efforts, or canister and flame throwers when weapons available in the front lines failed to solve tactical problems. On one occasion, General Harding wired from his advanced headquarters, "So many priorities on medical, engineer, anti-aircraft and other [supplies] are causing neglect of general ammunition and food for our fighting men."

Quartermaster officers in the field reported that the troops subsisted for almost a week on a daily diet of one-third of a "C" ration and one-sixth of a "D" ration,[5] equivalent to about 1,000 calories a day. Even when shipping space was available, the problem was not solved. Foods in glass jars were packed in paper cartons which disintegrated in the rain. The jars, unprotected by cartons, often broke. There was a shortage of packing equipment. Parachutes used for the drops had to be salvaged for further use. However, as the operation progressed, both headquarters and officers at the front learned by trial and error what was needed, in what quantity, and how to use efficiently the available transportation.

The establishment and maintenance of communications across the Owen Stanley Mountains and in the Buna area involved many difficulties. Shortage of space on the air supply line from Port Moresby limited delivery of equipment. Radio sets corroded or shortcircuited in the hot, moist air even when protected from the heavy rains. The more powerful radios used for communication between the front and Port Moresby worked well, but the limited Signal Corps staff was swamped with the coding and decoding of messages. Portable radios were often ineffective because the dense growth of trees and underbrush limited their range.

Headquarters at Simemi was connected with Dobodura, Hariko, and Oro Bay by teletype. Telephone wires were laid to each regimental headquarters, to the four air strips, to aircraft warning stations, and to all artillery batteries. Where jungle and swamp were absolutely impenetrable, reels were mounted on rafts and field wire was

---

[5] A "C" ration weighs 4.2 pounds and a "D" ration consists of three chocolate bars.

strung on trees as the rafts floated downstream. Altogether some 300 miles of wire were laid, all of it by hand and much of it under fire. On 23 December, 1st Lt. Philip S. Winson of the 32d Signal Company, while laying a battalion observation post telephone line, was with a platoon of the 126th Infantry which was isolated by enemy counterattack. For organizing the defense of several captured enemy bunkers, he received a citation.

Lines were frequently broken by enemy patrols or bombing. Native carriers innocently cut lengths of wire to tie up their bundles. Repair parties were sniped at by the Japanese in daylight, and at night were fired on by our own men, who were suspicious of any movement in the dark. However, communications were maintained effectively throughout the operation; few complaints were heard.

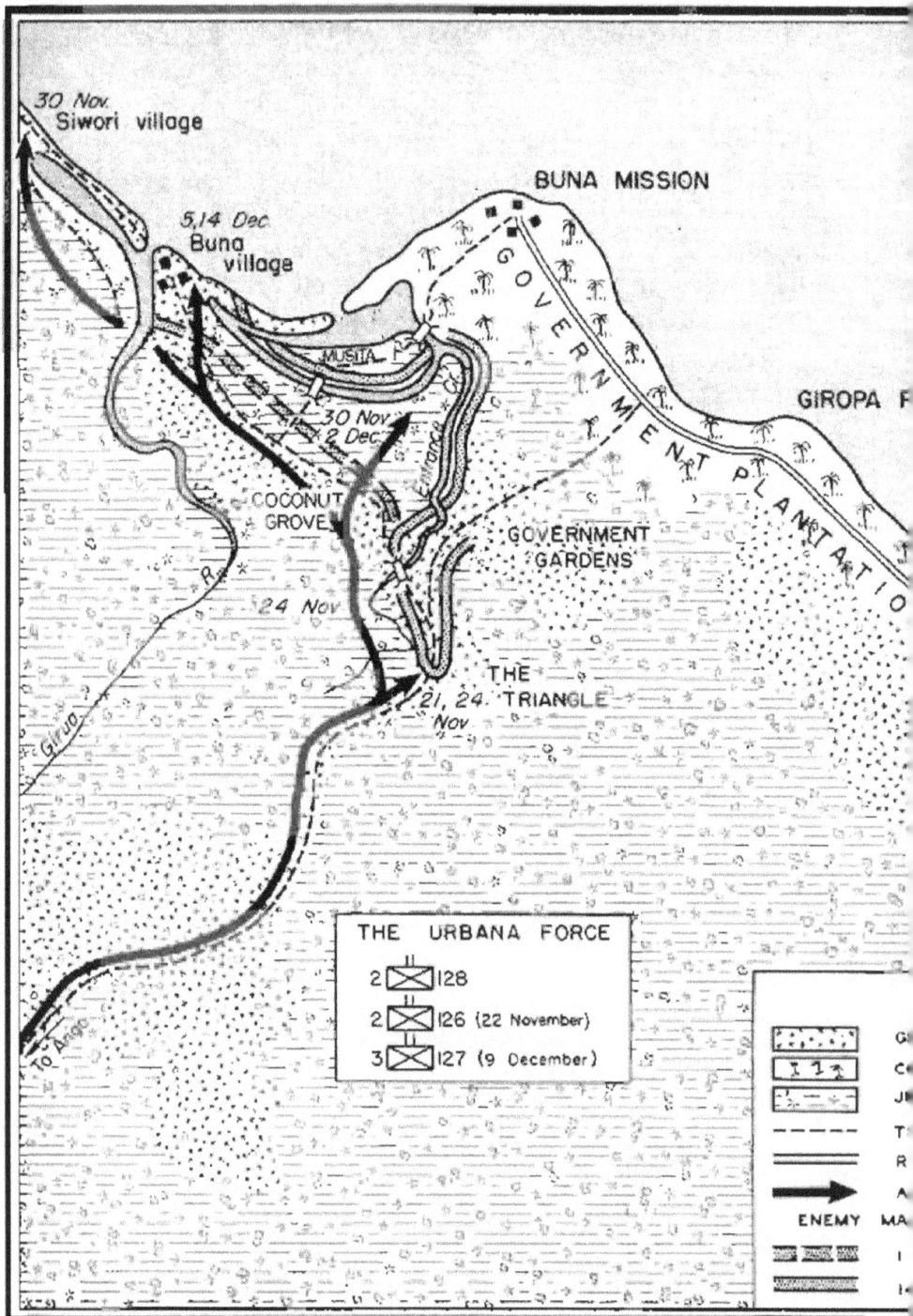

30 Nov.
Siwori village

BUNA MISSION

5,14 Dec.
Buna
village

GOVERNMENT PLANTATIO

GIROPA F

MUSITA

30 Nov
2 Dec.

COCONUT
GROVE

GOVERNMENT
GARDENS

24 Nov

THE
21, 24 TRIANGLE
Nov

Giruа R.

To Ango

THE URBANA FORCE

2 ⊠ 128

2 ⊠ 126 (22 November)

3 ⊠ 127 (9 December)

G

C

J

T

R

A

ENEMY MA

I

H

THE ATTACK ON BUNA

19 NOVEMBER————14 DECEMBER 1942

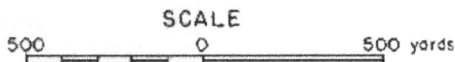

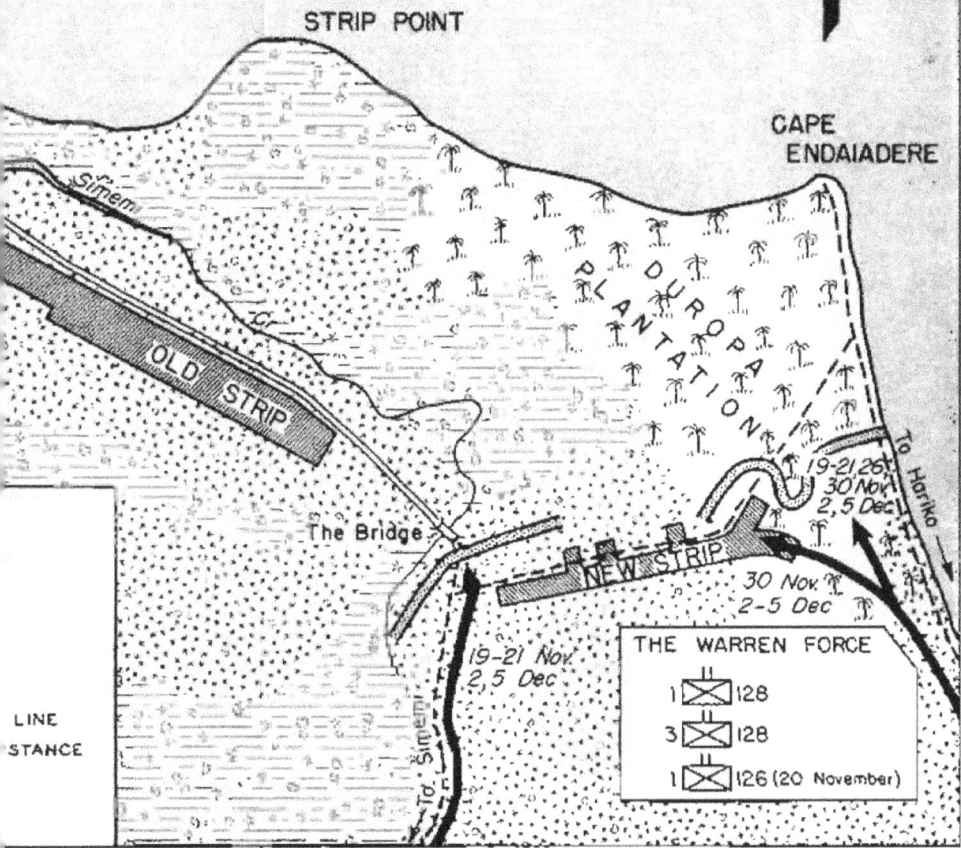

SCALE

500   0   500 yards

N

STRIP POINT

CAPE
ENDAIADERE

DUROPA
PLANTATION

Simemi

Cr.

OLD STRIP

To Hariko

19-21,26,
30 Nov.
2, 5 Dec.

The Bridge

NEW STRIP

30 Nov.
2-5 Dec

To Simemi

19-21 Nov.
2, 5 Dec

LINE
STANCE

THE WARREN FORCE

1 ⊠ 128

3 ⊠ 128

1 ⊠ 126 (20 November)

Cartographic Section, Diss. Unit by J.R. Hagan

Battering at Buna
[19 November—14 December]
(*Map No. 4, facing page 27*)

FIRST CONTACT

Early on 19 November the 1st and 3d Battalions, 128th Infantry, moved north in the rain along parallel trails to attack the Japanese forces on the east flank, which ran from the sea along the New Strip to Simemi Creek. C Company led the 1st Battalion up the coastal trail toward Duropa Plantation; the 3d Battalion, with K Company as advance guard, trudged along the track from Simemi village toward the New Strip. Both units advanced until they met rifle and automatic fire, then stopped. Ground observation was impossible; jungle and swamp limited expansion of the front and prevented direct communication between the two battalions. The 3d Battalion was about 500 yards southwest of the New Strip, and the 1st Battalion was approximately abreast on the coast. During the day, in the confusion of attack in the jungle, the leading units were completely out of contact with one another and had even lost contact within themselves. As night came on, rain was again falling. Our men could hear the sound of truck motors behind the Japanese lines, indicating that reinforcements were coming up; they could also hear the noise of pounding which suggested that the enemy was strengthening his defenses.

With this attack the Buna operation really commenced. It was not to be marked by broad strategic movements, for the terrain limited our action to a series of penetrations along well-defined corridors through the impassable swamps. During the first 26 days, our troops felt out the strength of the enemy's position, determined the general line of his well-camouflaged defensive works, and at the end of the period captured Buna Village. Our initial attempt to rush the enemy defenses had to give way to tactics of dogged infiltration by small groups, bunker to bunker, until the last stubbornly defended bunker was taken. Toward the end of December the introduction of light tanks and the weakening of the enemy forces speeded up the action, but throughout the operation it was the individual soldier's battle. Often cut off from his fellows by dense jungle underbrush, crawling on his belly in the sticky mud, each infantryman had to learn to fight alone.

Feeling out the Enemy Lines (20–25 November)

The disappointing results of the attack on 19 November did not destroy the confidence of our troops in a quick success, for Buna Mission was only 3 miles away. The 1st Battalion, 126th Infantry, arrived at the front during the 20th and went into the line on the right of the 1st Battalion, 128th Infantry, which by evening had pushed to the edge of Duropa Plantation. For the 21st, Division Headquarters ordered an all-out attack along the entire front, to be preceded by a bombing run of our planes along the enemy positions in the Plantation.

The front lines were so indistinct in the jungle that the bombing on the eastern front caused some casualties in the 3d Battalion, 128th Infantry, and damaged the morale of the entire unit. Apart from the failure of the air preparation, things went wrong, for the troops did not receive the divisional attack order until well after the bombing was over. The infantry attack was finally launched late in the afternoon, following another bombing raid and a mortar concentration. Units made slight advances, met well-directed fire from snipers, machine guns, and mortars, and then withdrew to their original positions.

On this same day, our first offensive against the western end of the Japanese stronghold also failed. The 2d Battalion, 128th Infantry, moved up west of the great swamp to take the place of the 1st Battalion, 126th Infantry (less three platoons of C Company and all of D Company), which, after its exhausting march over the mountains had been attached to the Australian 7th Division in operations west of the Girua River. The fresh battalion attacked up the Ango trail toward the junction where branches forked to the Mission on the right and to Buna Village on the left. As the point of the battalion approached this junction, the leader, Sgt. Irving W. Hall of F Company, spotted a Japanese machine gun 50 yards ahead. By cool action he got his men off the trail before the enemy opened fire, and the remainder of the battalion moved up on both sides of the trail against the narrow salient in the fork. At 1330,[6] enemy fire from the salient, later known as the Triangle, had stopped our troops. This area was to be the scene of some of the bloodiest fighting on the whole Buna front.

On 22 November the 2d Battalion, 126th Infantry, was released by the Australian 7th Division to the 32d Division and advanced along the Ango trail to support the 2d Battalion, 128th Infantry. This was the last major troop movement on the Buna front until reinforcements arrived. Henceforth, the 2d Battalions of the 126th Infantry and 128th Infantry were called the Urbana Force. Under the command of Col. John W. Mott, this force operated in the corridor west of the great swamp. On the east of that barrier, between Simemi Creek and the sea, the 1st and 3d Battalions of the 128th Infantry, the 1st Battalion of the 126th Infantry, and the Australian 2/6 Independent Company formed the Warren Force under Brig. Gen. Hanford MacNider. When this officer was wounded on the 23d, Col. J. Tracy Hale, Jr., of the 128th Infantry took over command of the Warren Force. Until 1 January, these forces were to fight separate actions, each with its own story.

The Urbana Force began an attack toward the Triangle on 24 November (Sketch No. 1, page 30). E Company, 126th Infantry, moved to the left flank and got 400 yards out into the swamp without meeting enemy opposition. By the next day it had struggled through the swamp to a point beyond Entrance Creek, close to the left-fork trail to the Village.

F Company, 128th Infantry, moved directly up the trail; E and G Companies, 128th Infantry, swung around the right flank. Enemy barbed wire and machine-gun fire stopped F Company at the apex of the Triangle. For a while the right-flank companies had easy going. Then, as they came out on the kunai-grass strip southeast of the Triangle, they encountered enemy fire. By dark it was clear that the enemy had drawn them into a trap on the relatively open ground, swept by fire from his fortifications. G Company lost its 60-mm mortars and light machine guns, and the men were forced

---

[6] Time used in this pamphlet is Melbourne time plus 1 hour.

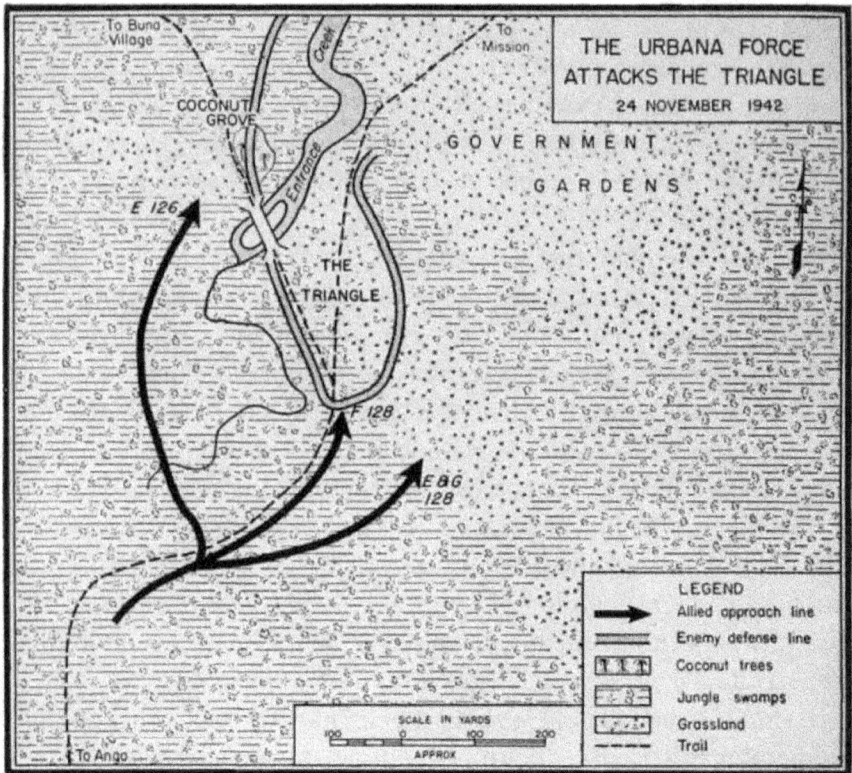

THE URBANA FORCE
ATTACKS THE TRIANGLE
24 NOVEMBER 1942

GOVERNMENT

GARDENS

To Buna
Village

COCONUT
GROVE

E 126

THE
TRIANGLE

128

E 8 G
128

LEGEND
Allied approach line
Enemy defense line
Coconut trees
Jungle swamps
Grassland
Trail

To Ango

SCALE IN YARDS
APPROX

Cartographic Section, Diss Unit by J.R.Hagan

into the swamp to the south. Ammunition ran low, and there was no food. During the night most of the company made its way back to the main force.

The day's fighting established clearly that the main enemy position in front of the Urbana Force was the deep narrow salient of the Triangle, commanding the Ango trail. Attack on the east side of this position was hampered both by swamp and by the open grass strip, where the enemy had excellent fields of fire, but the advance of E Company on the left suggested that the Triangle might be skirted on its western side. Consequently, attacks on the Urbana front during the next month were directed at the area west and north of the Triangle.

A WEEK OF ATTACK (26 NOVEMBER–2 DECEMBER)

On Thanksgiving Day, 26 November, the main action shifted to the Warren front, where our forces made a heavy attack, concentrat-

ing in a push northward through the Duropa Plantation. The 3d
Battalion, 128th Infantry, left I Company under Lt. Carl K. Fryday
to guard the Simemi trail, moved over to the coast and joined the
1st Battalion, 126th Infantry, to form the first wave. The 1st Battalion, 128th Infantry, followed 100 yards in rear of the left flank,

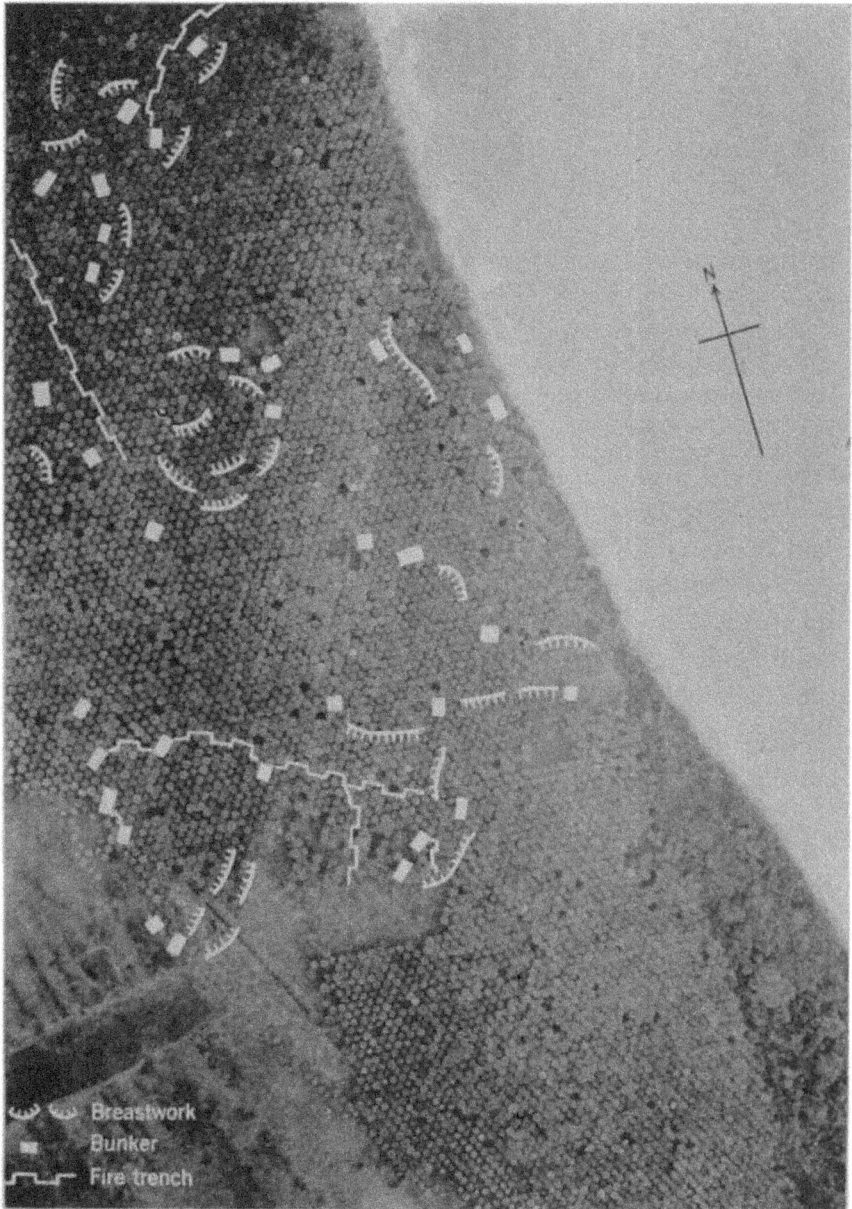

Japanese Defenses in the Duropa Plantation.

ready to push through and swing west. The frontage of the 3d Battalion, which made the main push on the coast, was about 400 yards; that of the 1st Battalion on the left was 800 yards; company fronts varied from 125 to 600 yards, depending on the opposition expected.

The attack of the 26th was the first in which the artillery could furnish real support. When the initial plans were made shipping had not been available for the transportation of artillery by sea; moving it by land over the mountains was obviously impossible; but by almost single-handed exertions, Brig. Gen. (now Maj. Gen.) Albert W. Waldron, Divisional Artillery Officer, managed to work some pieces forward by water and by air. On 26 November the following artillery had arrived:

Number of Pieces	Artillery	Unit
3	3.7-in. howitzers.......	Australian 1st Mountain Battery.
2	25-pounders...........	One troop, Australian 2/5 Field Regiment.
4	25-pounders..........	One troop, Australian 2/1 Field Regiment.
1	105-mm howitzer......	Battery A, U. S. 129th Field Artillery Battalion.

The artillery was divided between the east flank, on the coast north of Hariko, and the west flank in the vicinity of Ango, but the area of operations was so small that the fire of all guns could be concentrated at any point on the front. At first, however, the artillery was handicapped by inadequate maps and lack of ground observation. The flight of Australian Wirraway observation planes which had been brought up to Dobodura to meet this difficulty, did good work throughout the campaign in adjusting artillery fire. The pilots of the Wirraways were fearless in their hazardous job of hovering over enemy positions; one pilot even crept up on an unsuspecting Zero and downed it by one short burst.

Shortage of ammunition was also a problem. The original ammunition supply plan had to be given up by 7 December because of difficulties in transportation. Supply in predetermined quantities and types was then tried but abandoned on 17 December, partly because of frequent changes in requirements. Thenceforth ammunition was supplied through requisition by rounds of specific types, but always had to be used with the greatest economy. On 26 December the Australian 1st Mountain Battery ran out of ammunition and took no further part in the operation.

The Warren Force's attack on the morning of 26 November was preceded by aerial strafing and bombing. From 0730 to 0825, P-40's and Beaufighters strafed at tree-top level from the west end of the New Strip to Cape Endaiadere. A-20's bombed the rear areas from 0835 to 0853. These air attacks were followed by a half hour of pounding by the artillery, mortars, and machine guns. Everything proceeded according to schedule until the infantry jumped off at 0930. At once it became apparent that the supporting fires had not touched the enemy bunkers. Concealed machine guns and snipers opened up, and at nightfall our lines were in practically the same position as before the attack. Units of the 1st Battalion, 126th Infantry, had got close enough to the Japanese bunkers to see that the enemy machine guns were barricaded with oil drums and had a roof over them, but our troops did not yet fully understand the nature of the Japanese defenses.

A 3-day lull followed this repulse. On the Urbana front, units worked along the left flank to extend the line which E Company had previously established on the Buna Village trail. Active patrolling in this zone added to our scanty information regarding enemy positions.

On the 30th, the attack was renewed on both fronts. The Urbana Force made its main effort to the west of Entrance Creek. Units of this force moved up through the swamps during the night and jumped off before dawn against Buna Village. Within 100 yards they met machine-gun fire but pressed on despite heavy casualties, and by the end of the day they had made limited gains. In a wide flanking movement, F Company, 128th Infantry, reached Siwori Village and so cut enemy land communication between the Buna and Sanananda fronts. Other units got to the outskirts of Buna Village. On the right, E Company, 128th Infantry, advanced west of Entrance Creek toward Coconut Grove, which lies along the Buna Village trail just north of the Triangle. They failed to take the Grove, which was to prove almost as difficult to penetrate as the Triangle. In this action the 2d Battalion, 128th Infantry, captured the first prisoner taken in the Buna campaign.

The attack on the Warren front was not so successful. The plan for the 30th differed materially from that of 26 November, when two battalions had attacked northward in the Plantation. This time one battalion was to move west along the New Strip to deal with the opposition along its northern edge, and only one battalion was to advance north along the coast through the Plantation. The battalion in reserve would be ready to support either attack. Bren-gun carriers which had been counted on to spearhead the attack failed to arrive because of a shortage in shipping.

The infantry, attacking at dawn, made almost no progress. Leading the push north through the Plantation, A Company, 128th Infantry, ran into a log barricade on its right, while its left platoon was held up by automatic fire. It tried to knock out the barricade by mortar fire, but failed. Then a 37-mm gun was brought up for direct fire on the obstacle, but still the company could not advance. By noon the men were digging in where they were, and at nightfall B Company relieved them squad by squad.

Two companies of the 1st Battalion, 126th Infantry, pushed toward the eastern end of the New Strip but fared little better. C Company, advancing west on the south edge, was stopped when it was halfway along the strip by heavy fire coming from the north across the open field. It was apparent that Japanese defenses, concealed where the Duropa Plantation surrounds the spur which juts off northeast from the strip, commanded all the neighboring cleared ground. B Company reached the southeastern tip of the New Strip but got no farther.

At the conclusion of the attack on 30 November, the Warren Force had not penetrated the main line of enemy defensive positions, which was not to be cracked until tanks were employed on 18 December. Through the Duropa Plantation, from the sea to the north end of the little spur off the New Strip, the Japanese had a strong line of bunkers, each surrounded by individual emplacements linked with the main bunker by trenches. The western end of this line, just northwest of the spur, formed an almost impregnable strongpoint with fields of fire to the east across the spur, to the south across the New Strip, and to the west across the open ground north of the New Strip.

In many ways this strongpoint was the key defensive position in the Plantation area. As long as the enemy held it, the line to the coast could not be turned on its western extremity; frontal assault by infantry supported only by mortar and artillery fire proved unsuccessful time and time again. When the enemy defenses at the bridge on the Simemi-Buna trail over Simemi Creek were explored in the

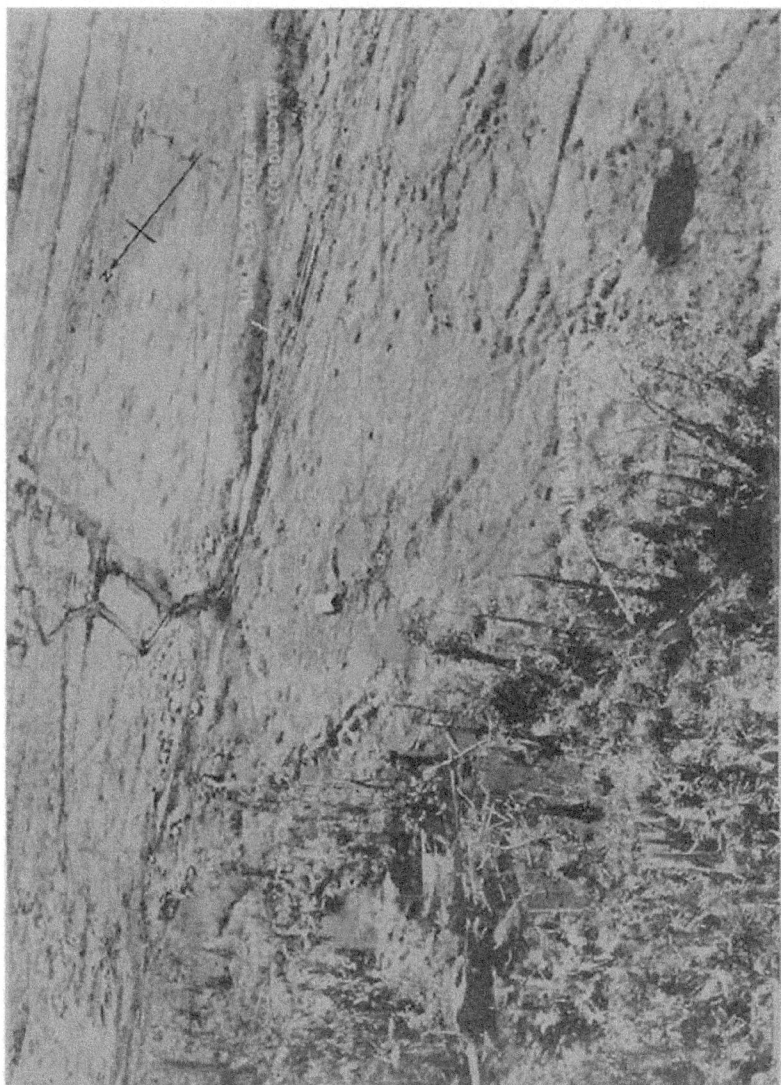

Terrain to the West of the New Strip.

next few days, it was discovered that another strongpoint had been constructed there. The cross fire between the bunkers at the bridge and the bunkers at the east end of the New Strip was to make attack north across the open ground of the strip so costly as to be impractical. Finally, Allied naval support was not available to carry out an amphibious landing farther up in the Plantation.

Meanwhile, a new commander for the forces attacking Buna was on the way. Lt. Gen. Robert L. Eichelberger, Commander of the U. S. I Corps, and staff officers landed at Dobodura on the morning of 1 December, after conferring with General MacArthur in Port Moresby the previous evening. At 1300 on the same day he assumed command of the Allied forces operating east of the Girua River.

The following morning General Eichelberger and his staff came to the front and watched another attack all along the line. The Urbana Force again attacked Buna Village and again failed, although G Company, 126th Infantry, under Lt. Cladie A. Bailey, mopped up a Japanese command post and supporting bunkers and then advanced our right flank to Entrance Creek. On the Warren front, the two main enemy positions, one at the bridge over Simemi Creek and the other in Duropa Plantation, stood as firmly as ever. B Company, 126th Infantry, got men within 25 yards of enemy positions in the Plantation. They could not penetrate the final protective lines, where they ran into well-coordinated machine-gun fire, and were forced to withdraw to the southeastern tip of the strip. At the Simemi bridge, A Company, 128th Infantry, tried grenades, 60-mm mortar fire, and infiltration, but could not reduce the bunkers or get men through the murderous cross fire of enemy light machine guns so sited that they swept the level terrain. At the close of the day the Japanese positions in the key areas were as strong as they had been when first assaulted on 19 November.

Even before the attack on 2 December, our troops were tired and dispirited, and this last repulse reduced their confidence to a low ebb, probably the lowest of the entire campaign. Two weeks of fighting had not even dented the Japanese line. Rations had been so short that troops sometimes received only one-sixth of a "C" ration per day. Torrential rain alternated with jungle heat. The insects seemed as determined as the enemy. Casualties from disease and wounds had reduced all battalions to approximately half strength.

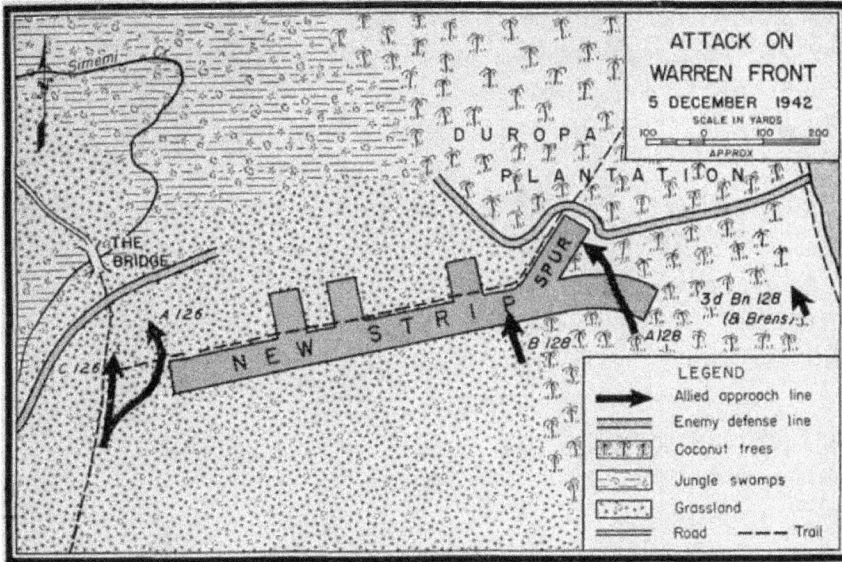

ATTACK ON
WARREN FRONT
5 DECEMBER 1942
SCALE IN YARDS
100   0   100   200
APPROX

LEGEND
→ Allied approach line
═ Enemy defense line
Coconut trees
Jungle swamps
Grassland
Road   ——— Trail

Cartographic Section, Diss. Unit by J.R.Hogan

BREAKTHROUGH TO THE SEA (3–5 DECEMBER)

Reorganization of the Allied forces in the Buna area and regrouping of units which had become badly intermixed during the fighting of the past 14 days followed promptly on General Eichelberger's assumption of command. Col. (now Brig. Gen.) Clarence A. Martin became commander of the Warren Force. The 1st Battalion, 126th Infantry, took over the lines on the Simemi-Buna trail south of the bridge; the 1st Battalion, 128th Infantry, occupied the Plantation positions; and the 3d Battalion, 128th Infantry, went into reserve on the coast behind the right flank. Minor reshuffling on the Urbana front was accompanied by the assignment of Col. John E. Grose as commander there. General Harding, Divisional Commander, was relieved by General Waldron. Elements of Headquarters, I Corps, were merged with Headquarters, 32d Division, and henceforth called Buna Force Headquarters, located near Simemi village. Headquarters of the Advanced New Guinea Force, under General Herring, who commanded all troops north of the Owen Stanley Mountains, was now at Soputa. Late in December it was moved to the neighborhood of Dobodura.

Reorganization of the supply system accompanied the front-line changes and began to show results in increased shipment of supplies

37

by air and water and quicker distribution to front-line units. The Bren-gun carriers, with Australian crews, arrived, and orders were prepared for an advance on the morning of 5 December. On the Warren front all three battalions were to take part. While two followed the Brens north through the Plantation, the third was to take the bridge over Simemi Creek (Sketch No. 2, page 37).

Early on the morning of the 5th, six A–20's made a bombing run from the Old Strip to Cape Endaiadere, and all the artillery in the Buna area concentrated its fire 500 yards ahead of our troops in the Plantation. At 0842 L Company, 128th Infantry, moved forward with the Brens on a 200-yard front while our machine guns strafed the trees to comb out the snipers. The presence of the Bren-gun carriers proved a complete surprise to the enemy, but he quickly rallied. As the Brens swung to the west to rake the enemy front lines, snipers in the trees picked off the crews from above; Japanese soldiers on the ground tossed hand grenades over the sides of the carriers. Within 30 minutes the Brens were immobilized. Fire from the front and from the strongpoint to the left pinned down the infantry, and by 1000 our men had withdrawn to their original lines. The Brens

Disabled Bren-Gun Carriers.
After the attack of 5 December in the Duropa Plantation.

lay deserted out in front and were stripped of their weapons by the Japanese before nightfall.

The 1st Battalion, 128th Infantry, moved up to the left of the 3d Battalion and attacked north across the eastern end of the New Strip toward the Japanese strongpoint. Under Lt. Samuel J. Scott, A Company made its way across the strip by noon and pushed on toward the spur. B Company under Lt. Milan J. Bloecher then went in on the left to cross the strip just west of the spur. At 1400 it had reached the south edge of the strip and set up its light machine guns on the left to protect the crossing. The soldiers crawled out in the fairly high grass, only to meet very heavy sniper fire when they reached a bare spot in the middle of the New Strip. The heat of the sun in the tall grass was terrific; the crack of a sniper's shot or a short burst from an enemy light machine gun followed any incautious movement. By 1700 the men of both A and B Companies were exhausted. At nightfall B Company reassembled on the south edge of the New Strip. The Antitank Platoon of the 1st Battalion, now constituted as a rifle unit, crawled up to relieve A Company in the Plantation just south of the spur.

The 1st Battalion, 126th Infantry, was meanwhile attacking the bunker area at the bridge over Simemi Creek. Fire from mortars and 37-mm guns forced the Japanese out of some of their positions east of the bridge. Then A Company and elements of C Company closed for an assault, but machine-gun fire on their left flank forced their withdrawal to a line about 200 yards south of the bridge. When artillery fire failed to reduce the enemy defenses, frontal attack was given up and B Company, relieving A on the line in the afternoon, tried to bypass the strongpoint by infiltrating across the creek southwest of the bridge. The attempt was frustrated by deep water and impassable swamp. No further gains were made during the day on that sector.

On the Urbana front, the 2d Battalion, 126th Infantry, was given the task of pushing through to the sea, thus cutting off Buna Village from the Mission (Sketch No. 3, page 40). The 2d Battalion, 128th Infantry, was to protect both flanks of the 126th. The infantry attacked at 1030 after an artillery and mortar concentration. For the first 30 minutes it met little opposition as it advanced cautiously through the jungle. Then the Cannon Company, 128th Infantry,

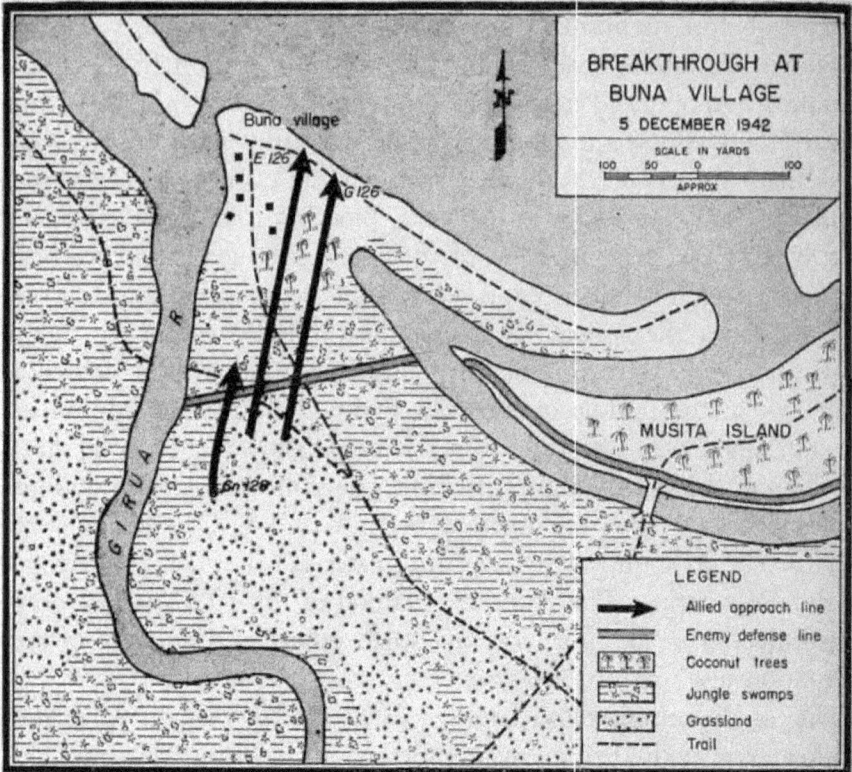

BREAKTHROUGH AT
BUNA VILLAGE
5 DECEMBER 1942

SCALE IN YARDS
100   50   0   100
APPROX

Buna village

E 126

G 126

Bn 126

MUSITA ISLAND

LEGEND
Allied approach line
Enemy defense line
Coconut trees
Jungle swamps
Grassland
Trail

Cartographic Section, Diss. Unit by J.R.Hogan

pushing ahead on the left along the Girua River, ran into mortar fire as it came out in the open. It stopped and sent a patrol toward the Village, but machine-gun fire almost at once pinned the patrol to the ground. Until late afternoon there was no further advance in this zone.

In the middle of the line, E Company, 126th Infantry, skirted the Village in such close contact with the enemy that little supporting fire was possible. G Company advanced on the right flank of E Company, and one platoon of G had driven to the sea by 1330. The platoon established itself on the beach between the maze of Japanese tunnel and pillbox positions at Buna Mission and another maze at Buna Village. Several enemy counterattacks were repulsed. By occupying this point, the platoon cut the Village from the Mission area, where the Japanese had a pool of troops and supplies to reinforce the Village. The platoon leader was German-born S/Sgt. Herman J. Bottcher, who had served in the Loyalist International Brigade in the

Spanish Civil War; for his outstanding accomplishment in this action he was made a captain.

General Eichelberger spent the entire day at the front; both his aide and General Waldron were wounded during the course of the attack. He sent two platoons of F Company to help E Company hold the line toward the Village. By nightfall the wedge to the sea was firmly established. For the first time since the campaign began, the Japanese line had been broken.

General Robert L. Eichelberger at the Front.

The Capture of Buna Village (6–14 December)

For the next week activity was very restricted. The Warren Force had thrown everything available at the enemy, again without success. Baffled and disheartened, it settled down in its positions. Gas stoves were brought up to provide hot meals, and the soldiers were permitted to have their pack rolls.

New tactics now were adopted. Artillery and mortar concentrations preceding earlier attacks had not succeeded in knocking out the Japanese defenses, partly because fire was directed too far behind the enemy front lines. The artillery preparation had served also to warn the enemy of impending attack. When the artillery opened fire, Japanese troops found relative security in their bunkers; when it ended, they crawled out into firing positions. Our infantry usually pulled back before the artillery concentration began and advanced after it ended to find the Japanese ready and waiting for them. Henceforth, the mortars fired at irregular intervals and only on targets located as accurately as possible. Patrols were pushed up to feel out any weak spots in the Japanese lines and so assist in inching our offensive forward by infiltration. Hand grenades were used more frequently as the firing slits and rear entrances of enemy bunkers were discovered. Although the success of these tactics was limited when measured in terms of advancing our lines, the patrol activity enabled us to fix the location of enemy bunkers and the persistent mortar fire wore down enemy strength and morale day by day. Prisoners of war reported that our mortar fire was extremely effective; all agreed that our mortars and artillery were more feared than air support.

Enemy counterattacks came from both flanks on the 6th, but the units on the Urbana front held tightly to their corridor. The next day they tried to take the Village. F Company, 126th Infantry, captured a trench at the edge of the Village, while G Company moved up to Coconut Grove. Early in the afternoon their battalion commander, Maj. Herbert M. Smith, was wounded. The greatly weakened companies on this flank could do little more than hold their positions. Further advance was impossible without reinforcements.

The needed reinforcements were provided. The 3d Battalion, 127th Infantry, under Lt. Col. Edwin W. Swedberg, finished its movement by air from Port Moresby to Dobodura and Popondetta on 9 December; on the 11th, it relieved the 2d Battalion, 126th Infantry, and on the following day began active night patrolling. On the morning of the 14th, after spending 2 days in the line to become acquainted with the location of enemy defenses and the nature of the terrain, I and K Companies, 127th Infantry, attacked Buna Village, following a mortar concentration of 400 rounds. Within an hour they had overrun the last enemy resistance in this area. Most of the enemy had retired before we advanced. The only American casualty was a souvenir-hunting soldier of the 126th Infantry.

On the same day the three battalions on the Warren front received new commanders: Maj. Chester M. Beaver for the 1st Battalion, 126th Infantry; Lt. Col. Alexander J. MacNab for the 3d Battalion, 128th Infantry; and Maj. Gordon M. Clarkson for the 1st Battalion, 128th Infantry. The Warren Force had improved greatly in morale during the comparative rest of the past week. It was soon to renew the attack.

SITUATION ON 14 DECEMBER

On the evening of the 14th the American line ran from the sea east of Buna Village roughly along the Buna Village trail, bending around the Coconut Grove and along the west edge of the Triangle to the Ango trail. After a wide gap covered by impassable swamp, our line began again with the jungle along Simemi Creek just south of the bridge bunkers and curved northeast across the western end of the New Strip. The open ground south of the New Strip between the bridge and the Plantation was constantly patrolled. At the eastern end of the New Strip our line looped northward to encircle a spur of the strip, then ran eastward through the Duropa Plantation to the sea.

Although heartbreaking setbacks, each with costly casualties, had thus far attended the campaign, our situation was actually improved to a marked degree. The 2d Battalion, 126th Infantry, had shown that the enemy lines on the west flank could be broken. The nature of the enemy defenses in the Plantation and bridge areas had become much clearer, even though our troops did not yet have the right weapon to smash them. The supply of the force was more effective; rear echelons now functioned with relative smoothness; command had been reorganized in all echelons; and most important, the troops had learned much from hard experience and were becoming battle-wise.

The enemy situation, on the other hand, had deteriorated considerably, though our soldiers were not yet aware of the fact. Each of our attacks had added to his casualties, the failure of long-promised reinforcements to arrive had sapped morale, and our aerial superiority had prevented supply except by parachute and by small coastal boats. After the last delivery by parachute on 10 December, the enemy supply situation grew ever more critical. His morale began slowly to crack. One Japanese soldier wrote in his diary:

With the dawn the enemy starts shooting all over. All I can do is shed tears of resentment. Now we are waiting only for death. The news that reinforcement had come turned out to be a rumor. All day we stay in the bunkers. We are filled with vexation. Comrades, are you going to stand by and watch us die? Even the invincible Imperial Army is at a loss.

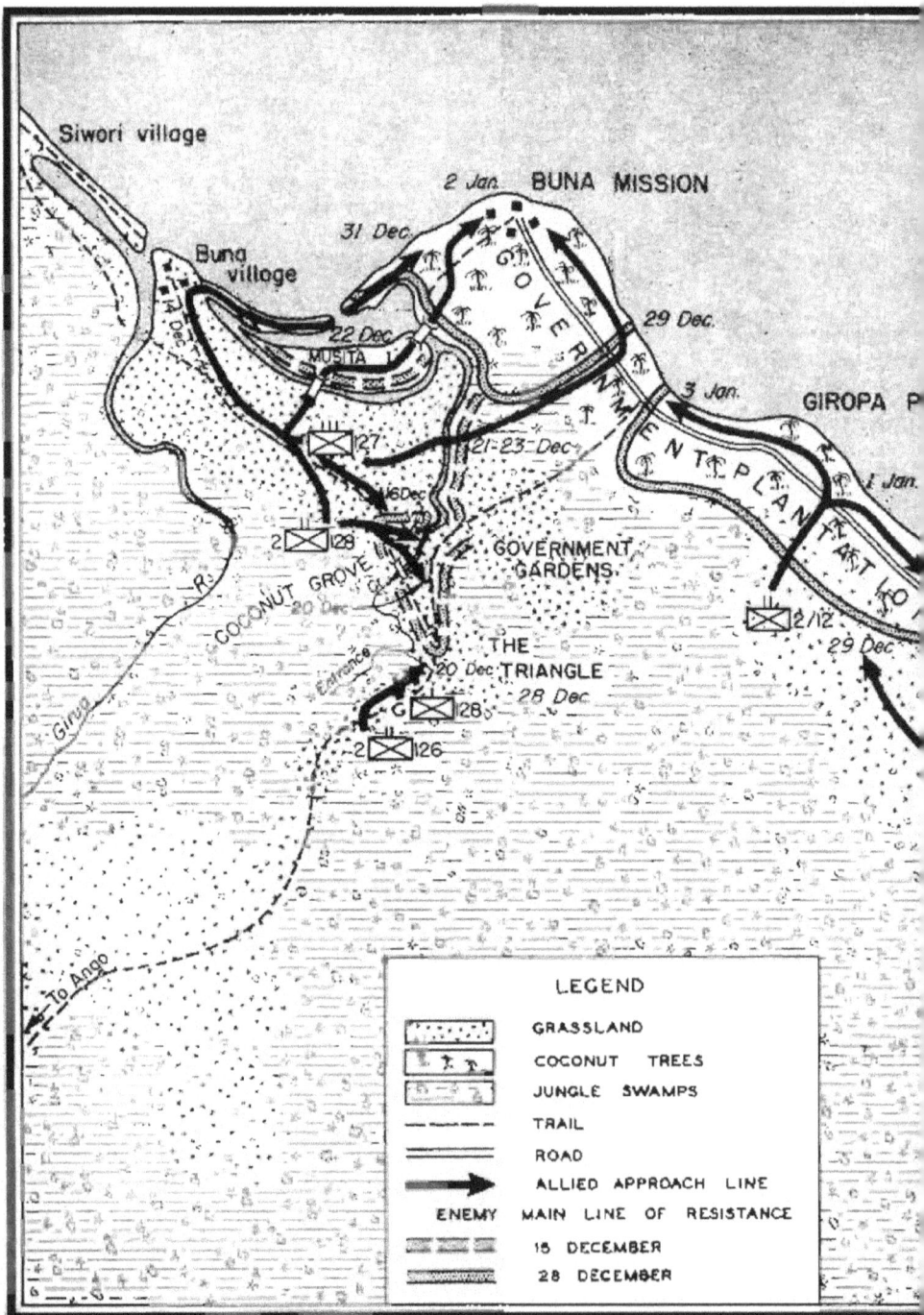

Siwori village

BUNA MISSION
2 Jan.

31 Dec.

Buna village

14 Dec.

22 Dec.

MUSITA

29 Dec.

GIROPA P

3 Jan.

21-23 Dec.

1/27

16 Dec.

2 128

GOVERNMENT
GARDENS

COCONUT GROVE
20 Dec.

1 Jan.

2/12
29 Dec.

Ginua R.

Entrance

20 Dec.

THE
TRIANGLE
28 Dec.

G 28

2 126

To Ango

LEGEND

GRASSLAND

COCONUT TREES

JUNGLE SWAMPS

TRAIL

ROAD

ALLIED APPROACH LINE

ENEMY MAIN LINE OF RESISTANCE

15 DECEMBER

28 DECEMBER

THE CAPTURE OF BUNA

15 DECEMBER 1942 ---- 3 JANUARY 1943

SCALE

500   0   500 yards

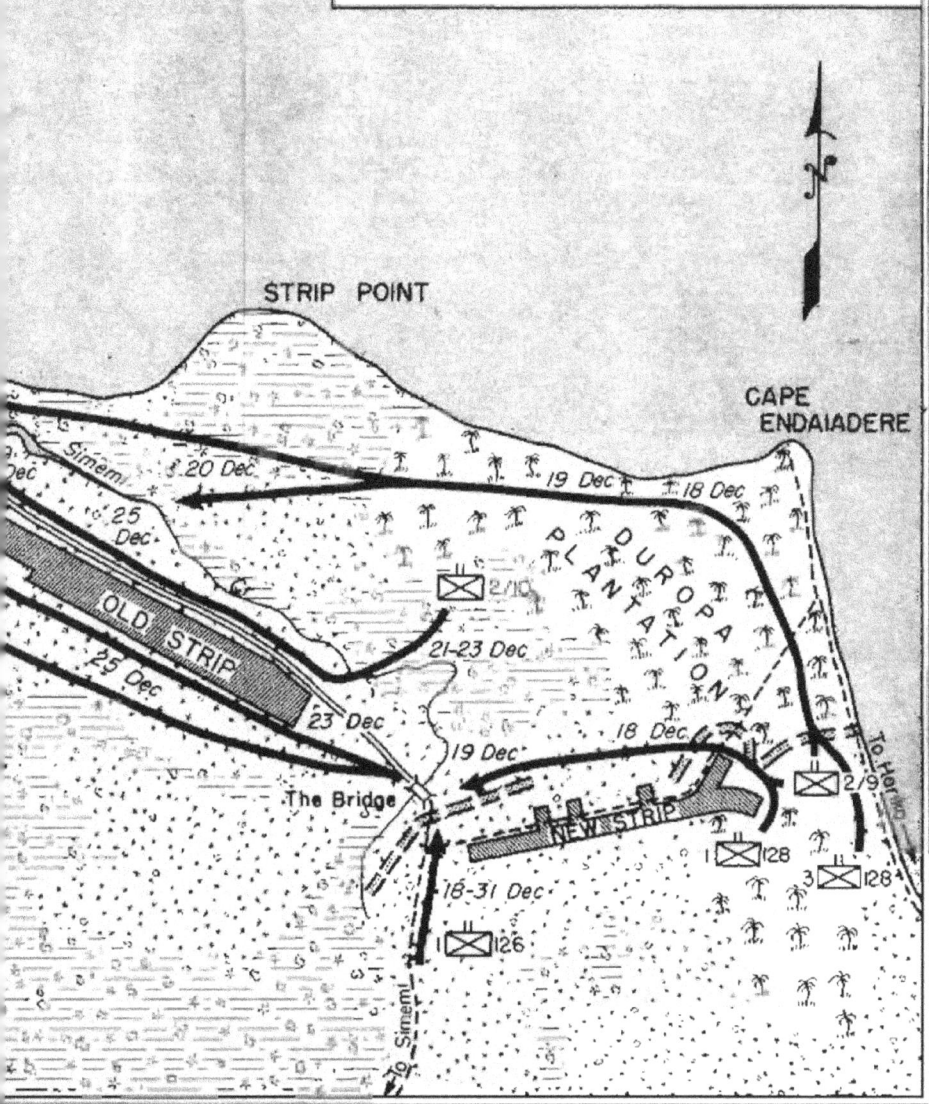

STRIP POINT

CAPE
ENDAIADERE

Simemi

20 Dec

25 Dec

19 Dec

18 Dec

DUROPA PLANTATION

2/10

OLD STRIP

25 Dec

21-23 Dec

23 Dec

19 Dec

18 Dec

To Hariko

The Bridge

18 Dec

2/9

NEW STRIP

1   128

18-31 Dec

3   128

1   126

To Simemi

Drawn in the Cartographic Section, Diss Unit by J.R Hagan

Warren Front: Capture of the Old Strip (15 December–3 January)

(*Map No. 5, facing page 45*)

Incessant attacks on both fronts characterized the final phase of the Buna operation. On the Warren front the Australian 18th Infantry Brigade,[7] seasoned veterans of Libya, Greece, Crete, and Syria, had come up in small boats from Milne Bay and with them came seven light tanks. Their commander, Brigadier (now Maj. Gen.) George F. Wootten, who was senior to Col. Martin, took over command of the front on 17 January. The next day, the Australian 2/9 Infantry Battalion, aided by the tanks, attacked northward along the coast, drove through the intricate network of the enemy defenses to Cape Endaiadere, and then swung west parallel with the shore. By the 20th our line ran along Simemi Creek from the bridge to its mouth. Here we were held up until the Australian 2/10 Infantry Battalion crossed the creek north of the bridge and outflanked the enemy positions in the bridge area.

An advance northwest up the Old Strip by one Australian and two American battalions brought our troops on 28 December to the final enemy position in the Government Plantation southeast of Giropa Point. On 1–2 January the Australian 2/12 Battalion and tanks crushed this last organized strongpoint on the Warren front.

The Tanks Break Through to Cape Endaiadere (18 December)

On 15 December the Warren front began to stir with preparations for an attack. During the next 3 days all three of the American battalions in the line edged forward until they were pressing tightly against the enemy all along the front.

---

[7] An Australian infantry brigade is equivalent to a U. S. infantry regiment.

On the 17th Brigadier Wootten assumed command. During the evening the seven General Stuart light tanks of X Squadron, Australian 2/6 Armored Regiment, rumbled up close to the front while mortars fired as rapidly as possible to conceal the noise of their motors. Later in the night a Japanese patrol alerted the front of the 1st Battalion, 128th Infantry, but moved off to the east without discovering anything.

Before dawn on the 18th, our troops in the Plantation withdrew 300 yards to allow the artillery to smash directly at the bunkers which the infantry had located in the advance of the past 3 days. During the 10-minute concentration by artillery and mortars, the Australian 2/9 Infantry Battalion under Lt. Col. Clement J. Cummings passed through the American units and worked its way toward the former front line. To insure complete surprise, these Australian units had been kept in rear areas until the actual time of the attack.

At 0700 the Australians jumped off. The artillery and mortars had wrecked the enemy front lines, and within an hour and a half, A and D Companies of the 2/9 Battalion, advancing with the tanks, had reached the Cape. They then swung west along the north coast but were stopped in front of a new line of Japanese bunkers which the artillery had not reached. Two tanks were knocked out by 13-mm antiaircraft pompoms, and after 1100 there was no further advance in this zone. During the afternoon the 3d Battalion, 128th Infantry, moved forward in the Plantation, mopping up and establishing an all-around beach defense south of the Cape.

C Company, 2/9 Battalion, attacked the enemy strongpoint at the spur of the New Strip. Enemy reinforcements were observed entering this ground in the morning, and the strongpoint put up stiff resistance throughout the day. Although tanks knocked out three or four bunkers with their 37-mm guns, the Australian infantry could not advance because of heavy fire from the remaining bunkers. Shortly after noon one tank was burned out in front of the 1st Battalion, 128th Infantry, which had been committed by this time on both flanks of C Company. Finally, in the late afternoon, the Australians began to work around the bunkers. Under the threat of being cut off, the enemy evacuated the strongpoint and fell back westward along the jungle north of the New Strip to the bunkers near the bridge. In the bridge area the 1st Battalion, 126th Infantry,

American Light Tanks Manned by Australians.

A tank stalled in the mud is being hauled out. Duropa Plantation, 21 December.

made no advance during the day, but artillery and mortar fire caused a considerable number of casualties among enemy troops in the vicinity of his bunkers.

Three of the tanks had been knocked out, and one-third of the Australians were casualties, but the Allied attack on the 18th had smashed once and for all the Japanese defenses in the Plantation. As our troops moved forward through the coconut trees, they found that the whole area was a mass of fortifications which the infantry alone could probably never have stormed. Some bunkers on the front line had roofs 3 to 4 feet thick; others had a layer of sheet iron on top and a front wall 6 feet thick. Surrounding them were individual covered fire pits with gun slits. These facts help to explain how the enemy defense had been able to stand up under our repeated attacks.

Our Troops Cross the Bridge (19–23 December)

On 19 December our line pushed about 300 yards westward through the Plantation along a 1,000-yard front. The following day the 2/9 Battalion and units of the 3d Battalion, 128th Infantry, advanced into the narrow nose of land on the north side of Simemi Creek. The 1st Battalion, 128th Infantry, which had followed the withdrawing enemy along the north edge of the New Strip, joined the 1st Battalion, 126th Infantry, in assailing the bunkers on the east side of the creek, and this time every one was taken. By noon of the 20th our troops were at the bridge.

The bridge over Simemi Creek might better be called a causeway, for it crosses more swamp than stream. The creek itself is only about 6 feet wide at the crossing, although over a man's head in depth, while the bridge is 125 feet long by 10 feet wide. Our troops found that the enemy had blown a gap of some 12 feet in the bridge over the main stream and commanded the crossing with 2 light machine guns, one .50-cal. machine gun, and 30 to 40 riflemen.

The 1st Battalion, 126th Infantry, spent the rest of the 20th and most of that night in attempting to get men across the creek. After the morning attack, units reorganized and in the early afternoon reconnoitered the bridge position. At 1650–1700 artillery and mortars laid down a concentration, and at 1700–1705 the mortars provided a smoke screen. Under cover of this, the pioneers brought up a catwalk,

Bridge over Simemi Creek.

After repair by the 114th Engineers.   New Strip in the background.

but it proved to be too short to span the gap. Enemy fire from the west bank on both sides of the bridge still raked the crossing, and the attack failed. Our forces were now facing along the creek from its mouth to the bridge, with the exception of a small tip of jungle at the very end of the nose. The 1st Battalion attacked the bridge again at midnight, B Company going single-file into the creek to the south of the bridge, but the leading platoon found the water too deep for wading and the enemy opposition as stiff as ever. Action was finally called off for the night, and Brigade Headquarters decided to outflank the bridge positions from the north.

On the 21st the Australian 2/10 Battalion, under Col. James G. Dobbs, which had come up by boat on the 19th, was put in the line along the creek north of the bridge. During the day some of its men worked their way across the swampy creek at the big bend due north of the bridge. More got across during the following day, and by the 23d the entire 2/10 Battalion commanded the bridge area from the north. Enemy defenders of the bridge area were now threatened with complete encirclement but put up determined opposition when the 1st Battalion, 126th Infantry, at last succeeded in pushing across the bridge immediately after noon and moved up the southern edge of the Old Strip. The 1st Battalion was now moving parallel with the 2/10 Battalion, which was advancing in skirmisher formation along the northern edge. Later in the afternoon the 1st Battalion, 128th Infantry, crossed the bridge and moved along the jungle south of the Old Strip as a left-flank guard. By nightfall our forward elements had advanced 800 yards from the bridge up the Old Strip, and the 3d Platoon of C Company, 114th Engineers, had completely repaired the bridge. It was now capable of carrying our light tanks. The 2/9 Battalion and the 3d Battalion, 128th Infantry, remained in the area between Simemi Creek and Cape Endaiadere to guard the coast.

THE FIGHT UP THE OLD STRIP (24–28 DECEMBER)

The three battalions west of the creek spent the next 5 days in fighting their way up the Old Strip. Until the very end of the campaign our troops always found that the Japanese, when pried out of one position, fell back into another just as strong or even stronger. The entire area of the Old Strip was commanded by a group of enemy bunkers at the northwest end of the runway; other bunkers dotted the northern edge and the center of the strip itself. On the 24th the tanks crossed the reinforced bridge over Simemi Creek and went in on the northeast flank. They found the going difficult. One overturned in a shell crater, and enemy 37-mm fire and Molotov cocktails had immobilized the rest by 1115. Nevertheless, our line had advanced about 500 yards by nightfall, except in the sector of the 1st Battalion, 128th Infantry, which was floundering in the swamp on the extreme south flank. After dark it was brought out and stationed in the open field behind the 1st Battalion, 126th Infantry.

Christmas was just another day. As one soldier wrote, "We hung out our socks and got water in them." For the units struggling on the open surface of the Old Strip it was a particularly uncomfortable day. Christmas Eve was marked by enemy bombing and the harassing fire of our mortars. After an artillery concentration at dawn, the infantry attacked, ran up against enemy bunkers, and recoiled to their original positions. C Company, 126th Infantry, spearheading the advance on the south side of the strip, was stopped by an extremely difficult bunker. One platoon of B Company swung around our right flank, and Col. Martin, commander of the 128th Infantry, took A Company around the left, but the bunker still stood at nightfall. Our line then consisted of an open V with the arms pointed up the Old Strip, the Australians on the right and the Americans on the left, with a strong enemy pocket between them.[8]

On the 26th our lines edged up a little as men of the 1st Battalion, 126th Infantry, outflanked and captured the bunker which had held them up the preceding day. A 25-pounder of the 2/5 Field Regiment was put into position in the vicinity of the bridge and fired armor-piercing shell with supercharge against the bunkers as they were definitely located. With this assistance the advance continued through the late afternoon of the 27th. By evening the upper end of the Old Strip had been reached, and our line began to swing around toward the north against the Government Plantation, which stretched along the coast from the mouth of Simemi Creek to Buna Mission. The 28th saw this pivoting movement completed; our line then pressed up against the Plantation and the dispersal bays at its southeastern edge bordering the Old Strip.

---

[8] The enemy bunkers and trenches in this pocket can be seen clearly on the photograph, p. 52.

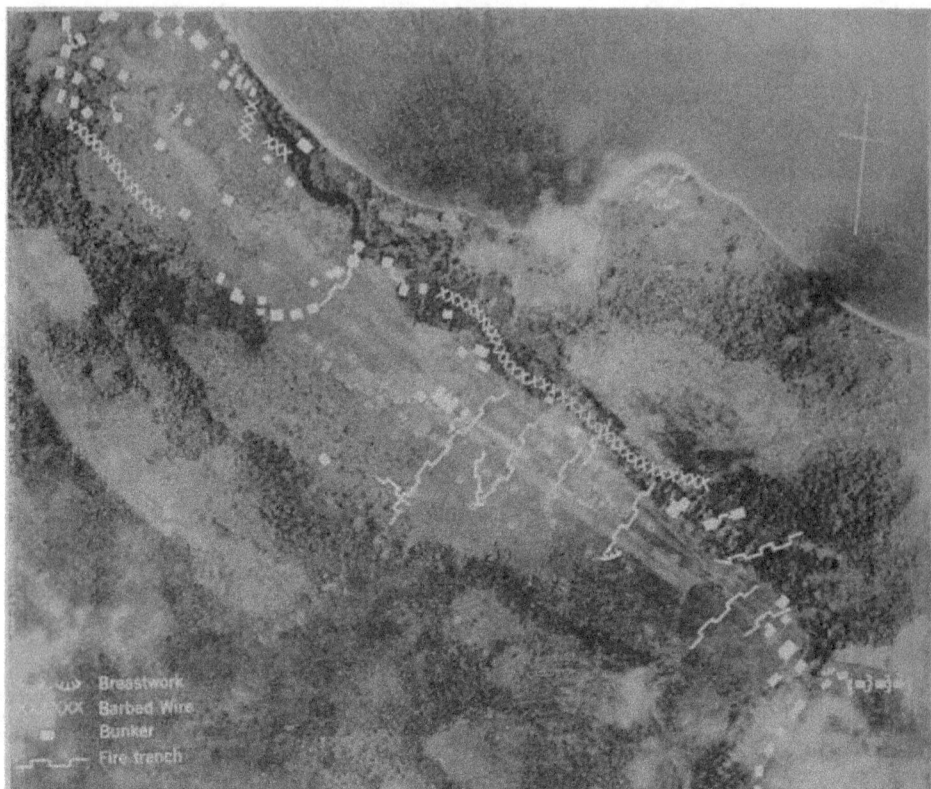

Defenses in the Old Strip Area.

THE LAST DAYS ON THE WARREN FRONT
(29 DECEMBER–3 JANUARY)

Throughout our advance up the Old Strip, the situation was even more fluid than was usual during the Buna operation. Enemy units were becoming disorganized and split up. Our own units had become intermixed, and small groups of Japanese were everywhere, dressed in American and Australian uniforms, using M–1 rifles, and calling out that they were Americans. On the night of 28 December, the situation was so confused that the enemy was able to penetrate to the command post of C Company, 128th Infantry, where a hand-to-hand struggle took place in the dark.

At the Government Plantation enemy resistance stiffened. Four new Allied tanks came up and led an advance on the afternoon of the 29th. They did not start from the intended jumping-off line and got out of touch with the infantry. As the tanks approached, the Japanese withdrew from their first line of defense to their second; then, while the tanks pushed on, they slipped back undetected to reoccupy their first line in time to stop our infantry. To prevent a repetition of the costly and unsuccessful attacks which had characterized the early fighting in the Duropa Plantation, our forces marked time until heavy reinforcements could be brought up.

On the 30th the 3d Battalion, 128th Infantry, took over the lines on the right opposite the dispersal bays, and on the 31st the Australian 2/12 Infantry Battalion, a fresh unit of the 18th Brigade, came in to the northwest of the 3d Battalion. More tanks arrived, and on 1 January the 2/12 Battalion under Lt. Col. Arthur S. W. Arnold made a thrust toward the sea across the north end of the enemy strongpoint. Within an hour of the jump-off the Australians were on the beach just southeast of Giropa Point. In the afternoon they moved south in the Plantation against the main center of enemy resistance. The 3d Battalion, 128th Infantry, closed in at the same time. By the evening of 2 January only two small enemy pockets remained. The next day the 1st and 3d Battalions, 128th Infantry, cleaned these out despite a last desperate stand by the enemy. Meanwhile, the 2/12 Battalion moved west to make contact with the Urbana Force.

Urbana Front: Capture of Buna Mission (15 December–2 January)

The action on the Urbana front, without tank support, moved forward less dramatically but with equal success. Buna Village had been taken on 14 December by the 3d Battalion, 127th Infantry. On 16 December the Coconut Grove was taken, but attacks against the Triangle from 17 to 20 December failed. In the course of the next 3 days, units of the 127th Infantry established a bridgehead on the east bank of Entrance Creek north of the Triangle, and on 24 December they began to push a wedge to the sea between the Mission and Giropa Point. By 29 December the wedge had been driven through. The enemy thus cut off in the Mission was assailed each day until 2 January, when the Mission fell. This ended the last organized resistance in the Buna area, but for the next few days it was necessary to mop up the whole region.

During the afternoon of 15 December, E and F Companies, 128th Infantry, attacked the Coconut Grove, which commanded the Buna Village trail northwest of the Triangle. By evening they had surrounded it, and the following morning they smashed through to Entrance Creek. Their battalion commander, Lt. Col. Herbert A. Smith, charged at the head of a squad to take one bunker; Sgt. Howard C. Purtyman of F Company led his squad to take another; Cpl. Daniel F. Rini of E Company captured a third bunker almost single-handed. During the mopping-up, Cpl. Rini was shot in the head by a wounded Japanese whom he was trying to aid. Thirty-seven enemy dead were buried.

The Triangle still commanded our best line of supply, the Ango trail; it was imperative to take this strongpoint before attacking the Mission directly. G Company, 128th Infantry, attacked up the trail on the 17th but lost 10 of the 27 men in the company within half an hour. During the night of the 18th, the 2d Battalion, 126th Infantry, moved up and shortly after daybreak on the 19th launched another attack. Thirteen A–20's dropped to tree-top level to plant almost 500 20-pound parachute bombs and to strafe the Triangle; then E and G Companies moved forward behind a rolling mortar barrage to within grenade distance of the enemy. Here enemy rifle, grenade, and small-mortar ("knee-mortar") fire met them. Capt. Boice, third commander of the battalion since Port Moresby, was killed in the action, and the battalion fell back. At 1600 another mortar concentration heralded a new attack, but the troops could not advance and dug in where they were. During the night the battalion was relieved. Thirty-four men, almost half the strength of the units involved, had been killed or wounded.

The 2d Battalion, 127th Infantry, under Lt. Col. Loren L. Gmeiner, had relieved the 2d Battalion, 128th Infantry, on the 18th and now put E Company in the lines at the Coconut Grove. On 20 December this company under Capt. James L. Alford attacked the Triangle from the northwest. Crossing Entrance Creek at 0845 under an artillery concentration, they tried to rush the position under cover of a smoke screen laid down by mortars. The attack failed. At 1230 they tried again. One platoon charged with grenades after the rest of the company had sprayed the region with tommy-gun and other small-arms fire, but the Japanese had evacuated the positions under fire and set up their automatic weapons to cover all approaches to the bunkers. The assault platoon, under Lts. Paul Whitaker and Donald W. Feury, was hit by enfilading fire and suffered many casualties, including both officers. E Company lost 35 men in the day's fighting.

Another Corridor to the Sea (21–28 December)

These gallant attacks made clear the extreme difficulty of taking the Triangle by direct assault. As a result it was decided to contain the Triangle, to cross Entrance Creek above the Coconut Grove, and to drive to the sea from there. Under cover of darkness on 21 December, K Company, 127th Infantry, pushed across the creek and established a bridgehead well to the north of the Triangle. This bridgehead was expanded by K and I Companies on the 22d; the same day a platoon of F Company crossed Entrance Creek to Musita Island in the lagoon at the mouth of the creek.

On the 23d the engineers finished a small footbridge across Entrance Creek at the edge of the Coconut Grove, and five companies of the 127th Infantry prepared to push to the sea along the track through the open field known as Government Gardens. The attack on the 24th started at 0615, but the units advancing behind a rolling artillery barrage soon lost contact with one another in the 5-foot-high kunai grass. On the right, I Company was held up by fire from enemy bunkers located along the right fork of the Triangle. During their attack, 1st Sgt. Elmer J. Burr lost his own life but saved his company commander by smothering the explosion of an enemy hand grenade with his body. At 0950 I Company, relieved by G Company, pulled back to reorganize. G Company took three of the bunkers but got no farther.

One platoon of L Company, split into patrols, broke through a weak spot in the defenses and got to the beach. Sgt. Kenneth E. Gruennert, leading one of these patrols, charged a bunker single-handed and put it out with hand grenades and rifle fire, killing three of the enemy. In the cover of this bunker he bandaged a serious wound in his shoulder and charged a second bunker. Its garrison fled from his grenades, but snipers killed him before the rest of his patrol could come up. Other groups followed, led by two officers. Lt. Charles

Bridge over Entrance Creek to Musua Island.

A. Middendorf was killed in the fight, and Lt. Fred W. Matz was wounded by our artillery, which did not know our troops had advanced so far. The Japanese closed in behind our forward elements, and after dark the surviving men withdrew, circling east of the enemy positions.

In a renewal of the attack on Christmas Day, first F Company under Capt. Byron B. Bradford, and then A Company under Capt. Horace N. Harger worked their way across the Government Gardens, crawling through the grass from bunker to bunker and knocking the garrisons out with grenades. They reached the Government Plantation in the vicinity of the road junction 700 yards southeast of the Mission, but the enemy attacked their rear and destroyed the Weapons Platoon of A Company. Two attempts to establish telephone communication failed. The problem during the heavy fighting of the next 3 days was to regain and maintain contact with this forward spearhead by clearing the enemy out of the north half of Government Gardens.

On 27 December General Eichelberger came up and directed the operation. A command group under Col. J. S. Bradley, Acting Chief of Staff, Buna Forces, undertook to establish a corridor to the 3 forward companies (A, F, and also B, which had just come up from Ango), now commanded by Major Edmund R. Schroeder. By the morning of 28 December this was accomplished. This action completely cut off the enemy in the Triangle, and a volunteer group from E Company led by S/Sgt. Charles E. Wagner and Pfc. James J. Greene, attacked this position in the evening. They found that the enemy had at last evacuated it. Examination of the Triangle disclosed no less than 18 bunkers, mutually supporting and connected by trenches.

The Mission Falls (28 December–2 January)

Even before the occupation of the Triangle, it was clear that the 127th Infantry had Buna Mission in its grip, but it took 4 more days to squeeze out the enemy. K Company attacked across the creek east of Musita Island on the late afternoon of the 28th, but the men who crossed in assault boats, unable to land in the face of heavy enemy fire, returned to our side. The weight of the attack was accordingly switched to the two ends of the arc about the Mission. On the 29th

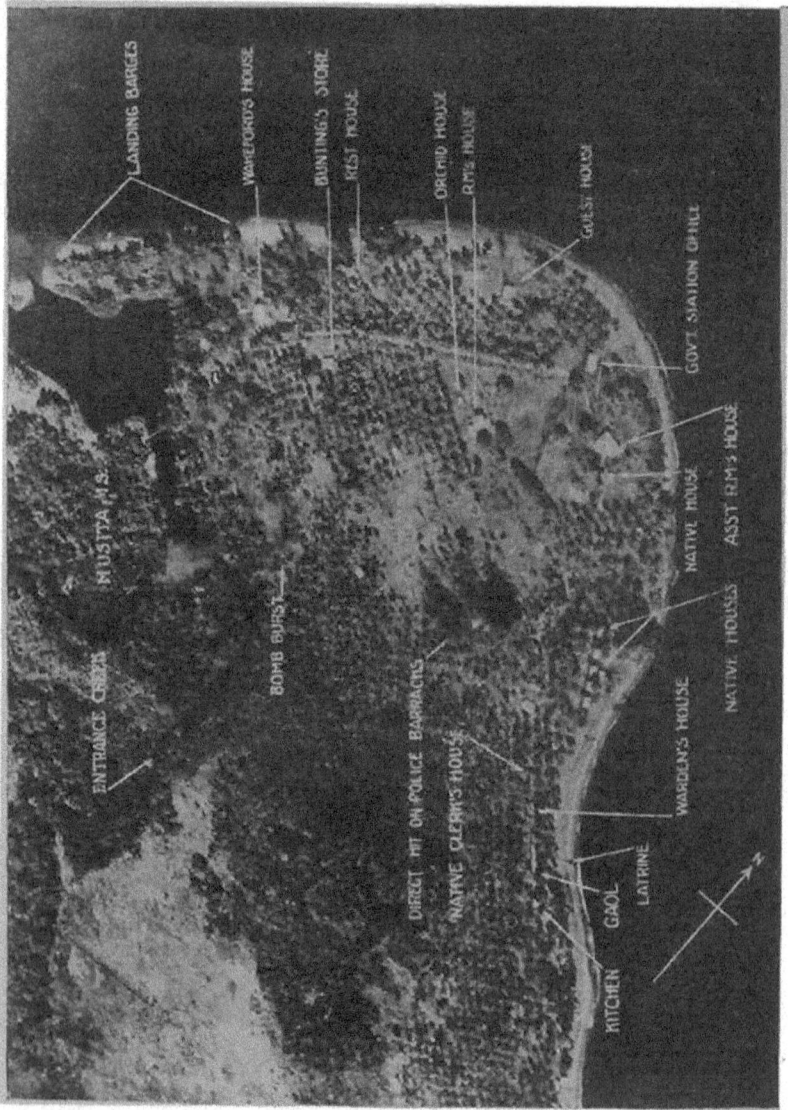

Buna Mission Area.

B Company extended the corridor southeast of the Mission to the sea and thus isolated the Mission from the enemy still holding out at Giropa Point. During the night of the 29th a patrol from H Company under Lt. Alan W. Simms waded across the mouth of Entrance Creek from the spit on the Village side to the spit on the Mission side and reported the crossing feasible. On 30 December, F Company, 128th Infantry, was moved up to Buna Village. A final assault was planned for the 31st.

Before dawn E Company, 127th Infantry, and F Company, 128th Infantry, began wading across and by 0500 had gained the spit on the Mission side without opposition. Then some of our troops advanced too far and alerted the enemy. E Company swung east but was unable to clear the bridgehead needed for G Company, 128th Infantry, which was to cross by the bridge at the east end of the island and attack northeast toward the Mission. The 1st Battalion, 127th Infantry, advancing on the right flank as the other jaw of the pincers, was held up along the beach.

Yet the end was not far off. A patrol of the 2d Battalion, 128th Infantry, made contact with the Warren Force on the 31st; on 1 January the 1st Battalion, 127th Infantry, could see our tanks in the vicinity of Giropa Point. All through the afternoon of the 1st, patrols in the neighborhood of Siwori Village kept reporting Japanese swimming from the Mission toward Tarakena.

On the morning of 2 January, the Urbana Force shifted its pressure to the corridor which it had forced through to the sea between Giropa Point and the Mission. G Company, 127th Infantry, under Capt. William Dames, swept forward on a 150-yard front in a final push up the coast. Many of the enemy attempted to escape an inevitable doom by taking to the sea, some swimming, others paddling small boats, rafts, and logs. These fugitives were machine-gunned by our coastal patrols and strafed by our planes. Meanwhile, the remaining Japanese were driven slowly up the coast through the desolate wreck of Buna Mission. The commander of the 1st Battalion, Maj. Schroeder, was mortally wounded, but the advance continued. By 1550, H Company had crossed from the island and was moving northeast; at 1600 G Company had reached the point of the Mission. Organized resistance was over. After 45 days of fighting, Buna Mission was ours. The Japanese force at Buna had been destroyed.

Of the original 2,200 men, 1,450 were captured or buried by our troops. Many others were buried by their comrades in the course of the battle. A few escaped into the jungle, where they starved or were hunted down. Still fewer succeeded in swimming to Sanananda, where they shared the fate of its defenders.

Offensive Action in Buna Mission.

Men of G Company, 128th Infantry, firing into Japanese bunker.

Buna Mission after the Battle.

Japanese Dead near Buna Mission, 3 January.

PART II–SANANANDA

Background of the Sanananda Operation

WHILE the right wing of the Allied force in Papua was carrying out the Buna operation, the left wing was attacking Japanese positions defending Sanananda, a few miles west of the Girua River. From these two bases the enemy had started his advance against Port Moresby along trails which converged at Soputa. The Allied counteroffensive was compelled by lack of good lateral communications in the waterlogged coastal plain to follow these same trails and was consequently split into two separate and parallel operations.

The bulk of the troops employed against Buna were American; the majority of those in the Sanananda zone were Australian, but American troops played a part out of proportion to their relatively small numbers. From the start of the operation, elements of the U. S. 126th Infantry were attached to the Australian 7th Division, which was under Maj. Gen. George A. Vasey, Allied Commander on this front. At the end of December the 163d Infantry of the U. S. 41st Division began to arrive from Port Moresby. After the fall of Buna, units of the U. S. 127th Infantry moved up the coast to the Sanananda front, while the tanks and the Australian 18th Infantry Brigade came by way of Ango Corner. The present account sketches only those general outlines of the Sanananda operation which are required for an understanding of American participation.

Japanese defenses west of the Girua River were in many ways stronger than those at Buna. They constituted a deep beachhead, roughly triangular in shape, protecting Sanananda harbor. The apex of this triangle was 3½ miles inland on the Soputa-Sanananda Road, the one good line of approach, and its base was anchored on strong-points covering the coastal trail between Cape Killerton to the west and Tarakena to the east. Gona was a flank position to the north-west of the main stronghold and could be reached from Soputa by a trail west of the road.

A group of mutually supporting positions at the apex on the Soputa-Sanananda Road covered the junction with the road of a branch trail to Cape Killerton. A half mile to the north was another group of positions where a second trail branched off toward Cape Killerton, and a half mile still further north was a third group of positions. Each defensive position consisted of a single ring of bunkers similar to those found at Buna, connected by fire and communication trenches and thus constituting a perimeter. Many of these perimeters were flanked by swamps and all were well concealed in the dense jungle.

Within the fortified area were concentrated some 3,000 survivors of the unsuccessful attack on Port Moresby, together with reinforcements which arrived by sea. Two of these units which had been deci-mated in the retreat across the Owen Stanley Mountains could be identified only tentatively: the Kusonose Butai and the Yokoyama Engineers. A third was definitely established as the Yasawa Butai. It consisted of 3 battalions of the 41st Infantry; the 1st Battalion was stationed at Gona, while the 2d and 3d were on the Soputa-Sanananda Road near its junction with the Killerton trail. On 20 November about half of the enemy troops were in positions along the road north of Soputa while the rest were on the coast.

Reinforcements arrived during the first 2 weeks of December. A detachment of the Yamagata Brigade, numbering less than 1,000 and consisting of the Brigade Headquarters, the 3d Battalion of the 170th Infantry, and 1 battery of mountain artillery, landed north of Gona during the night of 1–2 December. A second detachment of the same brigade, also less than 1,000 in number, landed near the mouth of the Mambare River on the night of 12–13 December. The total enemy strength in the Sanananda area was therefore between four and five thousand, at least twice the strength of the Buna garrison.

The Sanananda operation was conducted at first by the Australian units which had pushed the Japanese back across the Owen Stanley Mountains. But these units were too exhausted and too few to crack the strong defensive position of the enemy. Even after reinforcement by fresh Australian and American units, the attack was stalemated until the fall of Buna permitted the transfer of further Allied forces to the Sanananda front early in January. Thereafter the attack was pressed with unremitting intensity until the last Japanese pocket fell on 22 January 1943.

As the 16th Brigade of the Australian 6th Division and 25th Brigade of the Australian 7th Division came down to the southeastern coastal plain of New Guinea, they could look back on a series of uninterrupted victories since pushing the enemy out of Ioribaiwa on 28 September. Kokoda had fallen on 3 November; after a stand in front of Oivi, the Japanese had retreated without offering further battle. The Australians had pushed on toward the sea. On 19 November they made contact in Popondetta with an American patrol from the 126th Infantry, and patrols of the 25th Brigade entered Gona. These patrols were forced out of Gona by a Japanese counterattack before the main body of the brigade could come up.

On the same day the U. S. 126th Infantry under Col. Clarence M. Tomlinson was attached to the 7th Division to operate west of the Girua River. The 2d Battalion reverted to the control of the 32d Division on 22 November and fought with the Urbana Force, but the 3d Battalion and part of the 1st Battalion (C Company less one platoon, and all of D Company) remained on the Sanananda front until 9 January. The Cannon and Antitank Companies of the regiment, which had been in the vicinity of Juare, joined the Sanananda forces on 29 November.

The Road Block (22 November-9 January)

(Map No. 6, page 66)

A general attack was launched on 22 November. The Australian 25th Brigade moved against Gona on the west; the 16th Brigade attacked along the Soputa-Sanananda Road; the 3d Battalion, 126th Infantry, attacked on both flanks of the 16th Brigade to envelop the enemy. The frontal attacks of the 25th and 16th Brigades were unsuccessful, but on the Soputa road I and K Companies, 126th Infantry,

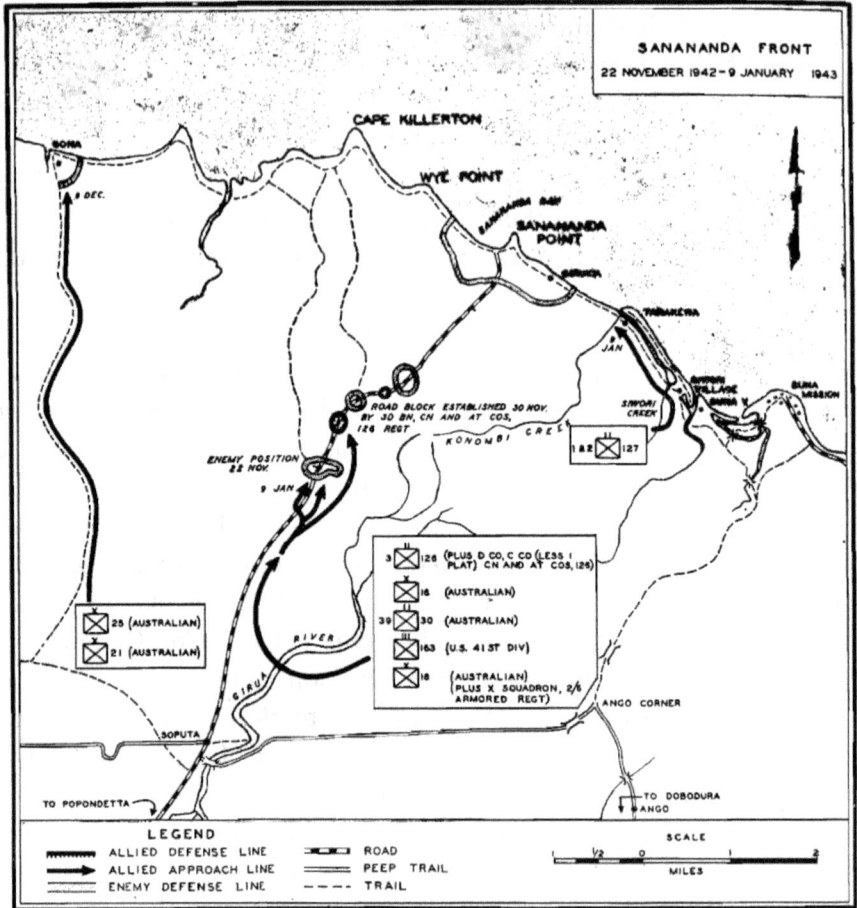

SANANANDA FRONT
22 NOVEMBER 1942 – 9 JANUARY 1943

managed to work part way around the enemy left flank, east of the road. During the next week they continued this envelopment, and the Cannon and Antitank Companies joined them. On 30 November, I Company under Capt. John D. Shirley and the Antitank Company under Capt. Meredith M. Huggins pressed on until they were astride the Soputa road in the rear of the enemy forward position, which was at the junction with the first branch trail to Cape Killerton.

At this point the American units established a road block to prevent use of the road to supply the enemy front. Operations of the next 3 weeks on the Sanananda front consisted essentially of the maintenance of this road block against desperate counterattacks from all sides. Sometimes enemy soldiers came so close to our trenches that our men could grab them by the ankles and pull them in, but they never broke through the block. Though K Company and the Cannon Company remained on the east flank through most of the period in order to maintain the supply line to the road block, it was often impossible to push supplies and ammunition through. Communications also were frequently interrupted. Day after day the dwindling survivors holding the road block had to spend all their daylight hours crouched in fox holes. Capt. Shirley was killed on 2 December. Capt. Huggins was wounded on the 5th but could not be evacuated until the 8th, when Lt. Peter L. Dal Ponte took command.

Against these odds, I Company and the Antitank Company held on until 22 December, when they were relieved by the Australian 39th Infantry Battalion (30th Brigade). They then joined other elements of the 126th Infantry on the main Sanananda front, south of the road block. Exhausted by the long period under constant fire, these units of the 126th Infantry were finally withdrawn on 9 January and rejoined the remainder of the regiment at Buna.

The Capture of Sanananda (4-23 January)

While the 126th Infantry had been holding the road block, the Australian 21st Infantry Brigade had come by air to Popondetta and reinforced the 25th Brigade on 28 November for a drive on Gona. They smashed through the desperate defense and captured Gona on 9 December. The Australians found that the last survivors of the enemy had fought with the dead bodies of their comrades decomposing about them. They buried 638 Japanese dead.

Fresh American troops also were arriving from Port Moresby. The 163d Infantry of the U. S. 41st Division under Col. (later Brig. Gen.) Jens A. Doe began to move by air to Popondetta and Dobodura on 30 December. The regiment was attached to the Australian 7th Division and assigned to the road-block positions. The 1st Battalion marched via Soputa to take over the positions of the Australian 39th Infantry Battalion from 2–4 January.

Moreover, operations at Buna were drawing to a close, permitting a shift of Allied strength. The 127th Infantry, operating on the western flank of the Buna front, had established an outpost in Tarakena Village, but on 4 January a Japanese attack drove it out. Next day the 1st and 2d Battalions counterattacked from Siwori Village. E Company, in the lead, advanced along a sandspit which lay just off the shore and directed enfilading canister fire from a 37-mm gun against the enemy on the mainland, who were slowly pushed westward through dense jungle by C and G Companies. These companies recaptured Tarakena on the 8th, and on the following day reached the bank of the rain-swollen Konombi Creek.

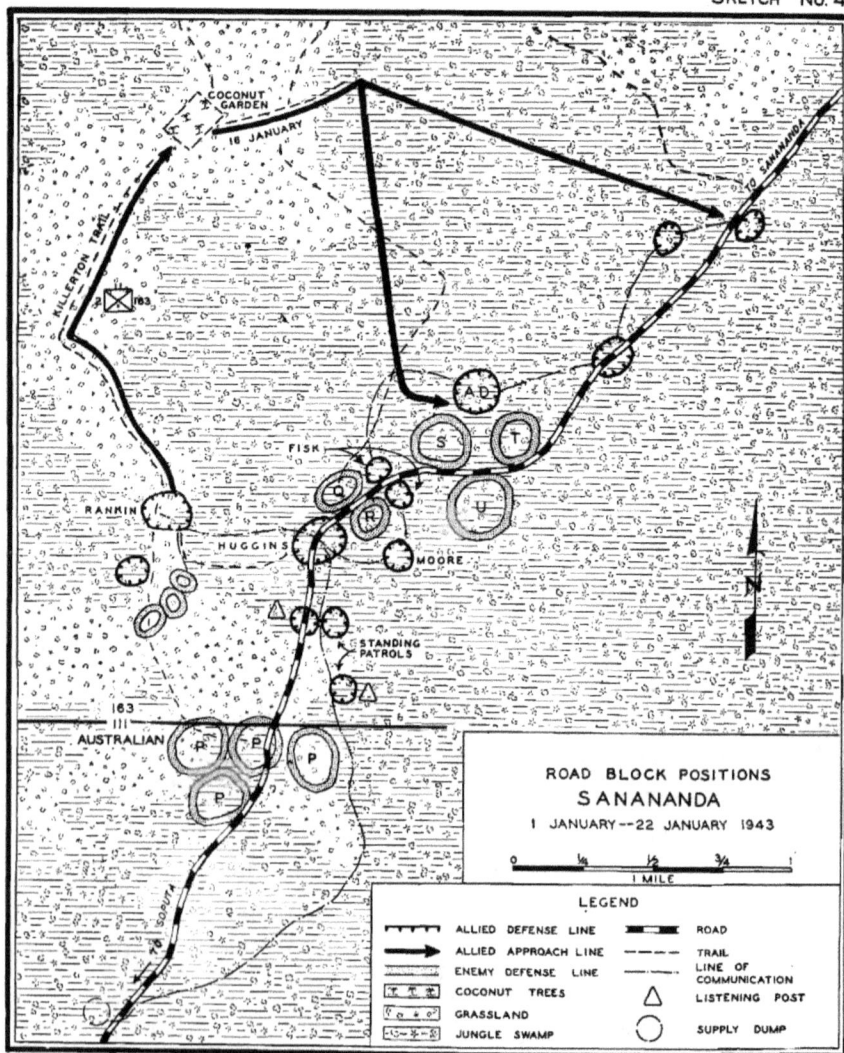

ROAD BLOCK POSITIONS
SANANANDA
1 JANUARY--22 JANUARY 1943

0   ¼   ½   ¾   1
1 MILE

LEGEND

ALLIED DEFENSE LINE		ROAD	
ALLIED APPROACH LINE		TRAIL	
ENEMY DEFENSE LINE		LINE OF COMMUNICATION	
COCONUT TREES	△	LISTENING POST	
GRASSLAND			
JUNGLE SWAMP	◯	SUPPLY DUMP	

Meanwhile, X Squadron, Australian 2/6 Armored Regiment, and the 18th Brigade were moving from Buna to the Sanananda front via Ango Corner. The 18th Brigade relieved the 30th Brigade and the units of the 126th Infantry on 9 January in the front line on the Soputa road. The Japanese at Sanananda could feel the net closing around them.

SITUATION ON THE SOPUTA–SANANANDA ROAD (4 JANUARY)
(Sketch No. 4, page 68)

With additional forces on hand, we could at last hope to break the long stalemate and sweep the enemy out of the Buna-Sanananda area. The Japanese position "P" at the junction of the trail to Cape Killerton with the Soputa-Sanananda Road had thus far held up our advance, but our maintenance of a road block to the north forced the enemy to rely on the roundabout and difficult Killerton trail for supply of his front. The whole situation along the road was quite extraordinary. Our original road block, about half a mile north of the enemy advanced position, was organized for all-around defense and called Perimeter "Huggins," after Capt. Meredith M. Huggins of I Company, 126th Infantry. Immediately north of Huggins was a second Japanese defensive position, and just beyond this a second Allied road block later called "Fisk," after Lt. Harold R. Fisk of the 163d. Less than a quarter mile farther north was a third group of enemy defenses. Our supply line to the road blocks ran through dense jungle east of the road and had to be patrolled constantly. At three points along it we maintained small defensive positions.

Perimeter Huggins was on relatively dry, jungle-covered ground, some 4 feet above the swamps on either side. An outer ring of rifle and automatic weapon positions extended about 250 yards from north to south and 150 from east to west. Each position was about 15 yards from its neighbors and consisted of fox holes for a squad. The fox holes were arranged in square or circular patterns. Between this and the inner or support perimeter were small supply dumps, kitchens, and lower headquarters. The inner perimeter, similar in plan to the outer, contained higher headquarters, switchboard, 81-mm mortars, ammunition dump, and aid station. Slit trenches were everywhere and the whole area was often densely crowded, especially when troops were in transit to other points.

Our other road blocks were, like Huggins, perimeters organized for all-around defense. When the 163d took over Perimeter Huggins from the Australian 39th and 49th Infantry Battalions and the Australian 2/7 Cavalry, Japanese tree snipers were very troublesome but were soon thinned out and forced back by harassing mortar fire, by special antisniper patrols, and by our own tree snipers. At night our men were not permitted to move from their slit trenches and those in the front line used hand grenades against suspicious noises. Huggins was our main position and headquarters of the regiment. Fisk consisted of two smaller perimeters, one on each side of the road. The enemy used no artillery or planes and his defenses were in such dense jungle that fear of casualties among his own men from tree bursts prevented effective use of his 40-mm mortars. Consequently, we had to deal only with small-arms fire and grenades.

The Japanese defenses consisted of groups of bunkers arranged about 5 yards apart in circular or oval patterns on both sides of the road.[9] Automatic weapons were sited to fire 6 to 8 inches above the ground and along fire lanes so carefully cleared that little disturbance of the jungle was apparent. Around the perimeters were trip wires and vines attached to warning rattles. Enemy patrols and snipers were active on all sides. During the 7 weeks of stalemate preceding the arrival of the 163d Regiment, American and Australian patrols had discovered that there were several Japanese defensive positions along the Soputa-Sanananda Road, but no clear understanding of their nature or extent had been gained.

Opening Up the Cape Killerton Trail (4–15 January)

Between 4 and 7 January, patrols found that just north of Huggins there were two enemy perimeters: "Q" on the west and "R" on the east of the road. At noon on the 8th, after a 15-minute preparation by artillery, mortars, and machine guns, B and C Companies attacked Perimeter "R." C Company attacked southward from the supply trail leading to Fisk but was stopped in front of "R" by a swamp which was more than waist deep as the result of heavy rain during the preceding night. B Company advanced northward from Huggins but had made only some 20 yards when it came under heavy cross fire. Here it dug in, about half way between Huggins and "R."

---

[9] A typical perimeter, known as "Q," which was on the west side of the road between Huggins and Fisk, is illustrated in Sketch No. 5, p. 71.

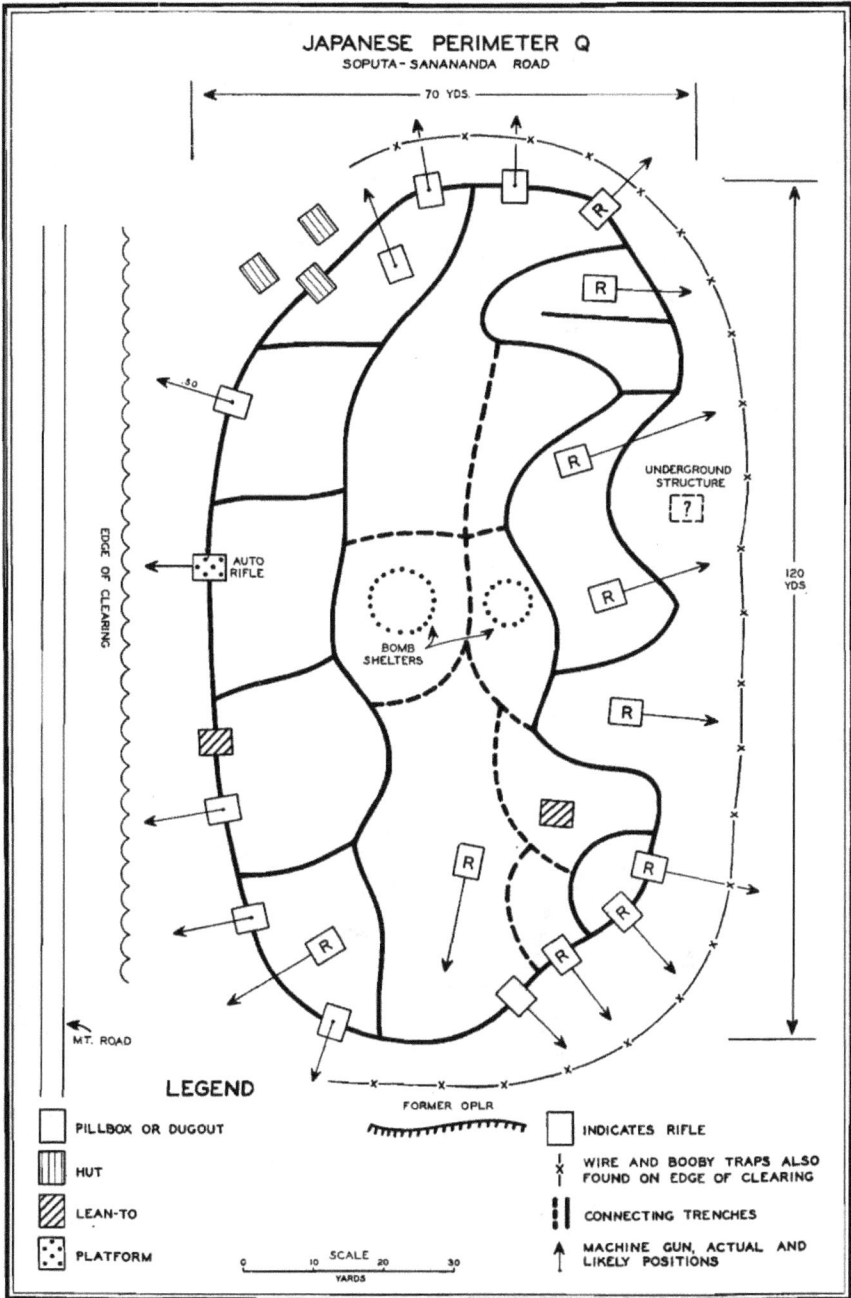

JAPANESE PERIMETER Q
SOPUTA - SANANANDA ROAD

LEGEND

☐ PILLBOX OR DUGOUT	⟆⟆⟆⟆⟆⟆⟆⟆ FORMER OPLR	☐ INDICATES RIFLE
⊞ HUT		WIRE AND BOOBY TRAPS ALSO FOUND ON EDGE OF CLEARING
▨ LEAN-TO		▮▮ CONNECTING TRENCHES
⊡ PLATFORM	SCALE	MACHINE GUN, ACTUAL AND LIKELY POSITIONS

The 2d Battalion had now come up and was bivouacked on the supply trail south of Huggins (Map No. 7, below). On the morning of the 9th, it was sent through Huggins a half mile due west to the Killerton trail, where it established under fire a road block cutting the enemy supply line to his advanced positions. This road block was called Perimeter "Rankin," after Capt. Pinkney R. Rankin of the 163d. The 2d Battalion's move was the first phase of a divisional plan of attack which was to employ both the 163d Regiment and the Australian 18th Brigade, now ready to advance. This plan directed the 163d to hold both possible lines of enemy retreat while the 18th Brigade was breaking through the southernmost Japanese defenses at "P." The 18th Brigade was then to drive up the Killerton trail to the sea and swing eastward along the coast to envelop the entire Sanananda defensive position. The 163d was at the same time to reduce the remaining enemy defenses along the Soputa-Sanananda Road.

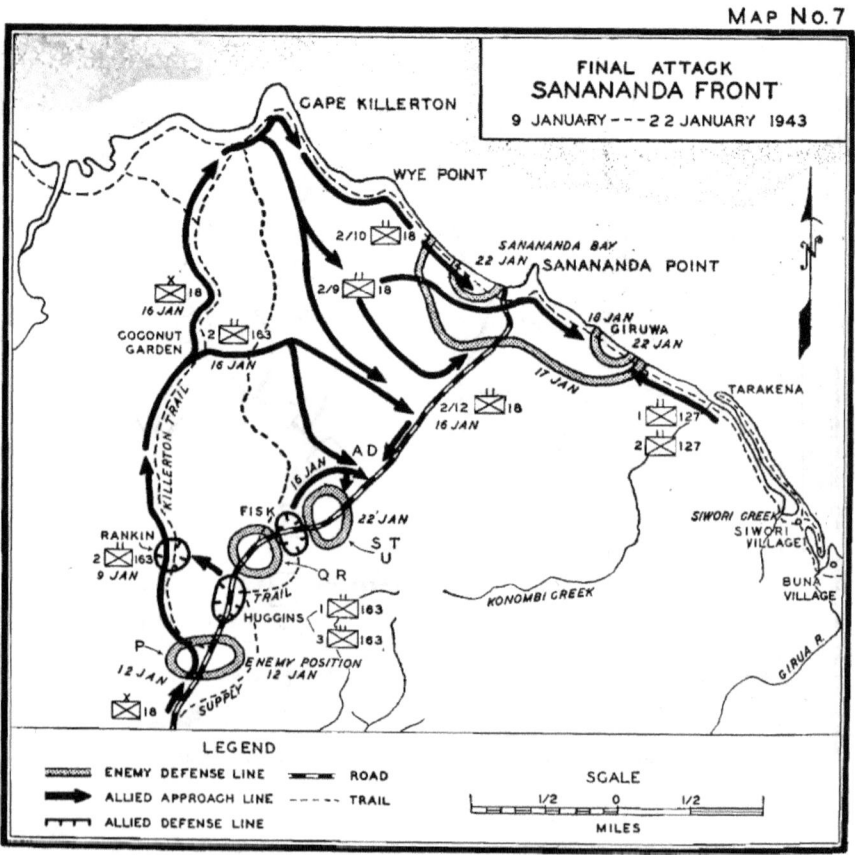

MAP No. 7

FINAL ATTACK
SANANANDA FRONT
9 JANUARY - - - 22 JANUARY 1943

LEGEND

ENEMY DEFENSE LINE   ROAD
ALLIED APPROACH LINE ----- TRAIL
ALLIED DEFENSE LINE

SCALE
1/2   0   1/2
MILES

Meanwhile, in the coastal area, the steady advance of the 1st Battalion of the 127th had been held up for a day by the Konombi Creek. In the early hours of the 10th, assault boats used in an attempted crossing had been swept out to sea by the swift current. That afternoon five men of C Company swam across the stream under enemy fire and rigged a guy wire which enabled the rest of the company, followed by A and B Companies, to cross in boats. By sundown, a bridgehead 200 yards deep had been established. The part of the 127th in the general plan of attack was to press northward through Giruwa Village and establish contact with the 18th Brigade.

During the next 3 days patrols from Huggins were active. On the 10th Perimeter "Q" was discovered to have been evacuated and was at once occupied by A Company, which sent out tree snipers and patrols to harass the enemy and feel out the contour of Perimeter "R," now open to attack from all sides. The 3d Battalion of the 163d was coming up along the supply trail. The Japanese could be heard and sometimes seen at work strengthening "R."

The 18th Brigade attacked northward on both sides of the road against "P" on 12 January, with the 163d providing diversions in the form of mortar fire directed against "R" and against enemy defenses on the Killerton trail south of Rankin. The Australians, aided by four light tanks, jumped off at 0800 after 15 minutes of concentrated artillery preparation. K Company of the 163d, operating southward from Huggins, covered the Australians' right flank. By noon it was evident that the attack had failed. Three of the four tanks, which attacked along the road, were out of action. One struck a land mine, one was stopped by two hits from an enemy 6-pounder gun, and the third bogged down when it turned off the road. During the afternoon, patrols from Huggins were sent at the request of the Australians to determine how far north the Japanese position extended.

Soon after daybreak on the 14th, a patrol of the 163d picked up a very sick enemy soldier in the bushes along the road just south of Huggins. Hustled to Australian 7th Division Headquarters for interrogation, the prisoner revealed that orders had been received on the night of the 12th–13th for able-bodied troops to evacuate "P," the southernmost Japanese position, leaving behind the sick and wounded. He had tried to follow, but was so weakened by malaria and dysentery that he could not keep up.

Acting on this information, the division ordered the 163d to send all available units southward to block escape routes but not to attack. K Company had remained just east of the road since the 12th, and B Company was sent from Huggins down the west side. These 2 companies moved south astride the road, and on the Killerton trail E and G Companies, after 100 rounds from the artillery and 200 from their 81-mm mortars, also moved southward. Nearly 100 Japanese were killed by this bombardment and by the infantry when it followed up. Meanwhile, the 18th Brigade renewed its attack and completely broke enemy resistance south of Huggins. For more than a mile north of its junction with the Soputa-Sanananda Road the Killerton trail was open. The first phase of the divisional plan of attack was now completed.

At 0730 on the morning of the 15th, a platoon of A Company, attacking from "Q," managed to get inside Perimeter "R" from the north without being detected. The rest of the company was at once pushed in. C Company, operating from Fisk, sent a platoon to press from the east. B, E, G, and K Companies were now released by the 7th Division from their southward movement and B was sent to the west side of "R" to complete the encirclement. Bunker after bunker was taken in attacks by small groups of our men using grenades, rifles, and submachine guns, but the entire perimeter was not captured until the following day. Shortly before noon, General Vasey came to Huggins and explained the plan for a second phase of the attack to begin next day.

The Envelopment (16 January)

The 18th Brigade, leaving the remnant of the enemy south of Huggins to be mopped up by reserve elements, was to move up the Killerton trail through the 2d Battalion of the 163d and carry out the envelopment of Sanananda. The 2d Battalion of the 163d was to cooperate by moving north from Rankin about 1½ miles along the Killerton trail to the Coconut Garden, where a branch trail connecting with the Soputa-Sanananda Road was believed to come in. After the Australian advance, the battalion would follow the branch trail east to the road, taking in the rear the enemy positions north of Huggins. The 3d Battalion, operating from Huggins and Fisk, was scheduled to complete the reduction of Perimeter "R." The 1st Battalion was to attack west of the road, enveloping Japanese positions known to be located north of Fisk. Two troops of Australian 25-pounders and two tanks were assigned to support the regiment and fifteen 81-mm mortars were massed in Huggins.

The units of the 127th Infantry which were advancing from Tarakena had meanwhile expanded their bridgehead north of the Ko-

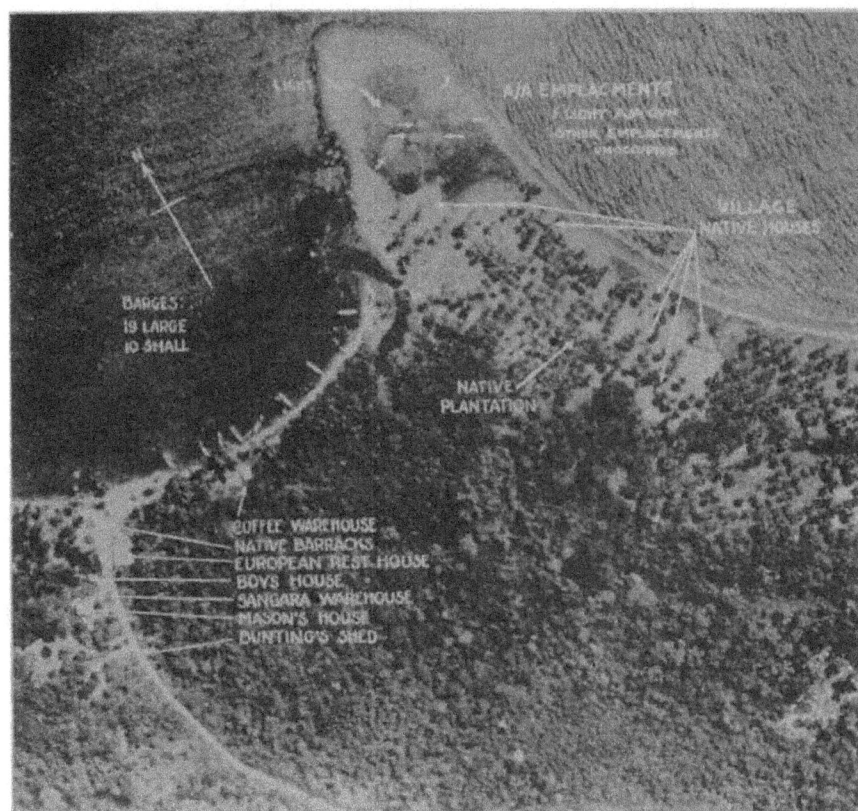

Sanananda Point.

nombi Creek. On 12 January patrols had got 700 yards beyond the creek, passing a string of apparently abandoned bunkers. These bunkers lay just inland from the beach and were scattered through an area about 150 yards in depth. On their return our patrols found that the enemy had reoccupied his bunkers. The patrols were withdrawn and C Company attacked, supported by artillery and mortar fire and a 37-mm gun using canister. Three of the bunkers were taken that afternoon. Active patrolling continued until the 16th, when the 127th was ordered to attack as part of the general plan of the 7th Division.

In preparation for the attack on the Soputa-Sanananda Road, A, B, and C Companies of the 163d, which had been squeezing "R," were relieved late in the afternoon on the 15th by I, K, and L Companies. During the night of the 15th–16th, the enemy north of Huggins was harassed by artillery fire. Then from 0845 until the jump-off at 0900, the artillery and mortars provided a heavy preparation while machine guns combed the trees and brush to the northwest of Fisk, where A, B, and C Companies were to advance around the right flank of the enemy positions and effect a junction with the 2d Battalion on the road. Soon after the jump-off, A Company on the right was pinned down by machine-gun fire from a Japanese perimeter at "S," but C Company, on the left, followed by B Company, met almost no opposition as it swung around to the road. Here at "AD" a perimeter bivouac was established. Company A, which had 20 heat-exhaustion casualties, was then withdrawn and sent to join B and C in the new perimeter. The two tanks, held in reserve for an emergency, were not used.

Meanwhile, the Australian 18th Brigade had advanced up the Killerton trail through the 2d Battalion of the 163d, which was now on its way eastward from the Coconut Garden toward the road. After some 800 yards, the trail followed by the 2d Battalion petered out and the troops began chopping their way through the jungle on a compass course aimed at the 1st Battalion objective. F and G Companies came out on the road just south of "AD" and were guided into the bivouac by a patrol from B Company. Part of H Company was left near the Coconut Garden to guard a trail junction, but the rest of the battalion chopped its way eastward to the road a mile north of "AD," where it made contact with patrols of the 18th Brigade's 2/12 Battalion, which had moved eastward from Cape Killerton along trails roughly parallel to the coast. The 2d Battalion had encountered numerous small parties of the enemy and killed over a hundred.

K and L Companies, operating northward from Huggins, had been squeezing "R," and in the early afternoon of the 16th mopped up this perimeter, from which most of the defenders had slipped out during the preceding night. Since the Australians had also cleared up the strongpoint at "P," all resistance south of Fisk was now liquidated. To the north the attack was making rapid progress. By evening of 16 January, the 18th Brigade, carrying out its wide envelopment, had pushed the 2/9 Battalion into the Sanananda perimeter. The 2/10 Battalion was left to face a stubborn enemy group on the coast west of the bay, while the 2/12 Battalion, advancing on the right flank, was on the road about a mile from the coast and in contact with the 2d Battalion of the 163d. On the coast, the 1st Battalion of the 127th attacked at 0800, following a rolling artillery and mortar barrage, but despite reinforcements from the 2d Battalion, made no progress in the face of effective enemy machine-gun fire. Pressure against this flank of the Japanese position was being maintained, to the obvious advantage of our operations elsewhere on the Sanananda front.

Any plan which the enemy might have had of an orderly withdrawal along the road to the beach at Sanananda had been foiled. His remaining forces were split up and under heavy pressure, short of ammunition and starving. The second phase of our attack had come to a successful end. The enemy himself realized that his few isolated strongpoints would soon be liquidated. During the night of 16–17 January, the higher Japanese officers removed their wounded from barges in which they set off to seek safety for themselves.

The Mopping-Up (17–23 January)

The exact nature of the remaining enemy defenses on the Soputa–Sanananda Road was not yet known, but a considerable force was believed to be between Fisk and Perimeter "AD." On the 17th, B Company probed southward from "AD" until it was stopped by fire from bunkers at "S." On the following day, C Company pushed forward east of B Company to envelop "S" but was stopped by fire from both flanks. Then A and K Companies extended the envelopment still further eastward but ran into another enemy perimeter at "T." F Company, ordered to join the attack on "T," advanced down the road from the north, disposing of 54 Japanese before it was held up by machine-gun fire from the northeastern end of Perimeter "T." About noon the enemy, caught between our 1st and 3d Battalions, showed their nervousness by opening fire on Fisk without being attacked.

Probing of the enemy defenses continued on the 19th, when a platoon of I Company, circling east and north from Fisk, ran into a Japanese perimeter at "U." F Company had by this time bypassed "T" and fought its way southward along the road to the north side of Perimeter "U." Reconnaissance in force had now explored the ground between our two main positions, and the general outlines of the three main enemy perimeters were known. Preparations were made for an attack on the 20th, intended to overrun the three perimeters from south to north, beginning with "U." Just after noon, the 25-pounders fired 250 rounds on the target area while the mortars in Huggins fired 750 rounds, and the machine guns of M Company from Fisk combed the trees and brush. Just as this preparation ended and I Company was poised to rush forward from the south, a mortar short killed Capt. Duncan V. Dupree and 1st Sgt. James W. Boland, while a sniper got one of the platoon leaders. The company hesitated for a moment, then went in to attack, but the effect of the bombardment was lost. The enemy had slipped out of his bunkers into firing positions and our attack was stopped.

Next morning at 1035, A and K Companies followed closely a perfectly timed concentration of artillery, mortar, and machine-gun fire into Perimeter "T," breaching the defenses and fanning out inside. This softened the resistance in front of B and C Companies which were facing "S," and all 4 companies were able to sweep south to the road by 1120, mopping up both "S" and "T." Our shell fire killed many Japanese and kept the rest inside their bunkers until our infantry were close enough to throw grenades into the firing slits and entrances or shoot down survivors as they crawled out like rats from a hole. After this attack 525 enemy dead were counted. Many showed evidence of starvation and disease. Outposts were placed along the road and most of our troops returned to Perimeter "AD" for supplies and rest.

Just before daybreak on the 22d, 31 Japanese, the remnant of 500 fresh troops landed 10 days earlier near Giruwa, were killed in front K Company's bivouac on the road. A lone prisoner reported that some 200 of this outfit had been lost through battle casualties near Sanananda and through disease; a group sent to reinforce the defenders of the road positions had arrived too late; he and his companions had been trying to escape westward.

At 1047, I and L Companies attacked "U" from the south, moving in with the last mortar salvo of a heavy bombardment. They found the resistance weak and by 1300 made contact with E Company, which had replaced F Company on the east side of the perimeter. We had 1 man killed and 1 wounded, whereas 69 Japanese were killed by our infantry and many more by our artillery and mortars. Enemy fleeing northward were picked off by our patrols, and general mopping-up continued through the 23d.

The 18th Brigade had meanwhile reduced 2 Japanese perimeters on the coast between Killerton and Sanananda and 2 more at the north end of the road. The 127th Infantry had been making steady progress toward Giruwa. On the 18th it gained 300 yards along the beach, but had trouble clearing the enemy out of swampy jungle on its left. There the terrain prevented use of the 37-mm gun against bunkers, so .50-cal. machine guns were used with good effect. Pressure was kept up, and by 1630 on the 20th we were within 300 yards of Giruwa Village. Next morning the advance continued against rapidly weakening opposition and the Village was taken by noon. Just beyond it, contact was established with the Australians. Early

A Fox Hole on Giruwa Beach.
Men of the 127th Infantry holding a position reached on 20 January.

in the afternoon a large Japanese hospital area was discovered 300 yards inland. Prisoners stated that some 2,000 casualties of the retreat over the Owen Stanley Mountains had been there late in November, but all save 200 had died from lack of medical care or from starvation.

On 22 January, the 127th completed the mopping-up. By that evening 46 prisoners had been evacuated to Buna; a total of 69 were taken in the Giruwa area. The Japanese defenders of Sanananda, like those at Buna, had been destroyed. The Buna-Sanananda operation was ended.

CONCLUSION

THE BUNA-SANANANDA operation may seem a small show when judged by the standard of operations in other theaters. The Allied forces which took part were the Australian 7th Division, reinforced by two brigades, the U. S. 32d, and a regiment of the 41st. They fought on the defense to remove the threat of enemy land attack on Port Moresby. They killed over 5,000 Japanese soldiers and marines, the total enemy force in the area of operations. But this is not the whole story. The men who fought in the stinking swamps of Papua have special grounds for pride in their victory.

They met the enemy in positions which he had chosen deliberately and fortified cunningly, and they crushed him. Their victory, like the victory on Guadalcanal, proved that the Japanese could be beaten in jungle fighting and that the vaunted Japanese morale could crack. Though the Buna-Sanananda operation was defensive in the larger sense, it was nevertheless a tactical offensive and a fitting prelude to the Allied offensive of 1943 in the Southwest Pacific.

Our troops fought the enemy, and they fought the jungle. They learned the bitter lessons of jungle warfare. Each day the heat, the humidity, and the diseases of the jungle sapped the strength of those who did not fall, killed or wounded. As one example, the units of the 126th Infantry which went into the action on the Sanananda front had 1,199 men and officers; when these same units were relieved on 9 January 1943, only 165 men and officers came out of the lines. They had fought their way foot by foot through tangled swamp and kunai grass around the Japanese position; for 3 long weeks they had held their road block despite incessant attacks from the strong enemy forces which they kept apart. Of these and of all the men in the Buna-Sanananda operation, it can be said, "They accomplished their mission."

Annex No. 1

Comparative Table of Strength and Casualties—Buna-Sanananda Operation

Regimental combat teams	Strength entering combat zone	Casualties				
		Killed in action	Other deaths	Wounded in action	Sick in action	Total casualties
32d Division:			*26 September 1942–28 February 1943*			
126th Infantry............	3,791	266	39	816	2,285	3,406
127th Infantry............	2,734	182	32	561	2,813	3,588
128th Infantry............	3,300	138	29	557	2,238	2,962
41st Division:			*2–23 January 1943*			
163d Infantry...........	3,520	85	16	238	584	923
(Plus estimated strength)....	300 3,820					
Total.........	13,645	671	116	2,172	7,920	10,879

Annex No. 2

Decorations

(Medal of Honor, Distinguished Service Cross, Legion of Merit, Silver Star, and Oak Leaf Cluster only)

The following list of decorations is based on the best records available to date but is not necessarily complete. The list is arranged alphabetically by name, showing rank, arm or service, residence, organization, station, and date of citation. Posthumous awards are indicated by an asterisk (*).

Medal of Honor

1st Sgt. Elmer J. Burr,* Inf., Wisconsin, 32d Division, Buna, 24 December 1942.

Sgt. Kenneth E. Gruennert,* Inf., Wisconsin, 32d Division, Buna, 24 December 1942.

Distinguished Service Cross

Lt. Col. Bernard G. Baetcke, Inf., Michigan, 32d Division, Sanananda, 30 November 1942.

Capt. Cladie A. Bailey, Inf., Indiana, 32d Division, Buna, 2 December 1942.

Lt. Col. Chester M. Beaver, GSC, South Dakota, 32d Division, Buna, 5 December 1942.

Capt. William F. Boice,* Inf., Indiana, 32d Division, Buna, 19 December 1942.

Capt. Herman J. F. Bottcher, Inf., California, 32d Division, Buna, 5–11 December 1942.

Col. Joseph S. Bradley, GSC, South Carolina, 32d Division, Buna. 28 December 1942.

Col. John J. Carew, CE, Massachusetts, 32d Division, Cape Sudest, 16 November 1942.

1st Lt. James T. Coker, Inf., Oklahoma, 32d Division, Tarakena, 8 January 1943.

1ST LT. JOHN W. CROW,* Inf., Texas, 32d Division, Buna, 19–20 November 1942.

CAPT. PETER L. DAL PONTE, Inf., Michigan, 32d Division, Sanananda, 9 December 1942.

COL. GEORGE DE GRAAF, QMC, Texas, I Corps, Buna, 5 December 1942.

BRIG. GEN. JENS A. DOE, USA, California, 41st Division, Sanananda, 21–22 January 1943.

2D LT. JAMES D. DOUGHTIE, CE, Massachusetts, 32d Division, Buna, 23 December 1942.

1ST LT. JAMES G. DOWNER,* Inf., Kentucky, 32d Division, Buna, 9 December 1942.

MAJ. DANIEL K. EDWARDS, Inf., North Carolina, I Corps, Buna, 5 December 1942.

CAPT. POWELL A. FRASER, Inf., Georgia, 32d Division, Tarakena, 11 January 1943.

2D LT. TALLY D. FULMER, Inf., South Carolina, 32d Division, Buna, 31 December 1942–11 January 1943.

MAJ. MILLARD G. GRAY, Inf., Indiana, I Corps, Buna, 25 December 1942–1 January 1943.

COL. JOHN E. GROSE, Inf., West Virginia, I Corps, Buna, 2 January 1943.

CAPT. HAROLD E. HANTLEMANN, Inf., Iowa, 32d Division, Buna, 1–3 December 1942.

1ST LT. JOHN E. HARBERT, Ord., Michigan, 32d Division, Cape Sudest, 16 November 1942.

LT. COL. MERLE H. HOWE, GSC, Michigan, 32d Division, Buna, 5 December 1942.

CAPT. MEREDITH M. HUGGINS, Inf., Oregon, 32d Division, Sanananda, 1 December 1942.

1ST LT. JAMES I. HUNT, Inf., Ohio, 32d Division, GHQ, SWPA, 2–5 December 1942.

1ST LT. JOHN R. JACOBUCCI, Inf., Wyoming, 41st Division, Soputa, 21 January 1943.

1ST LT. THOMAS E. KNODE, Inf., North Dakota, 32d Division, Buna, 5 December 1942.

2D LT. PAUL R. LUTJENS, Inf., Michigan, 32d Division, Buna, 5 December 1942.

Lt. Col. Alexander J. MacNab, Inf., Vermont, 32d Division, Buna. 10 December 1942–3 January 1943.

Capt. Robert P. McCampbell, Inf., Nebraska, 32d Division, Buna, 27 December 1942.

Lt. Col. Melvin L. McCreary, FA, Ohio, 32d Division, Buna, 24 December 1942.

Col. William V. McCreight, GSC, Wisconsin, Hq U. S. Forces Buna, New Guinea, 1 December 1942–25 January 1943.

Brig. Gen. Clarence A. Martin, GSC, South Carolina, 32d Division, Buna, 3 December 1942–5 January 1943.

2d Lt. Fred W. Matz, Inf., Wisconsin, 32d Division, Buna, 24 December 1942.

1st Lt. Erwin J. Nummer, Inf., Michigan, 32d Division, Buna, 30 November 1942.

1st Lt. Herbert G. Peabody, Inf., Vermont, 32d Division, Cape Sudest, 16 November 1942.

Lt. Col. Walter R. Rankin, Inf., Montana, 41st Division, Sanananda, 14 January 1943.

Col. Gordon B. Rogers, GSC, California, I Corps, Buna, 5 December 1942.

Capt. Donald F. Runnoe, Inf., Michigan, 32d Division, Buna, 2 January 1943.

Maj. Edmund R. Schroeder,* Inf., Wisconsin, 32d Division, Buna, 27 December 1942.

2d Lt. Paul L. Schwartz, Inf., New York, 32d Division, Buna, 5 December 1942.

Lt. Col. Herbert M. Smith, Inf., Wisconsin, 32d Division, Buna, 7 December 1942.

2d Lt. John E. Sweet, Jr., Inf., Pennsylvania, 32d Division, Buna, 26 December 1942.

Brig. Gen. Albert W. Waldron, Inf., New York, 32d Division, Buna, 5 December 1942.

Lt. Col. Simon Warmenhoven,* MC, Michigan, 32d Division, Soputa, 26 November 1942.

Capt. James W. Workman,* Inf., Texas, 32d Division, Buna, 24 December 1942.

Lt. Col. Roy F. Zinser, Inf., Wisconsin, 32d Division, Buna, 16 December 1942.

PFC. WALTER A. BAJDEK, Inf., Michigan, 32d Division, Buna, 10 December 1942.

PFC. WILLIAM BALZA, Inf., Wisconsin, 32d Division, Buna, 25 December 1942.

PFC. HERMAN BENDER,* Inf., Wisconsin, 32d Division, Buna, 31 December 1942.

PVT. JACK M. BINNS,* Inf., Michigan, 32d Division, Cape Endaiadere, 26 November 1942–11 December 1942.

PVT. ROBERT H. CAMPBELL, Inf., Iowa, 32d Division, Buna, 17 December 1942–1 January 1943.

S/SGT. CARL J. CHERNEY,* Inf., Wisconsin, 32d Division, Buna, 20–21 November 1942.

PVT. JOHN E. COMBS, Inf., Tennessee, 32d Division, GHQ, SWPA, 1 December 1942.

PFC. JACK K. CUNNINGHAM, Inf., Texas, 32d Division, Tarakena, 11 January 1943.

S/SGT. DELMAR H. DANIELS,* Inf., Michigan, 32d Division, Buna, 1 December 1942.

TEC. 5 EDWIN C. DE ROSIER,* MD, Michigan, 32d Division, Buna, 19 November 1942.

PVT. HOWARD M. EASTWOOD,* Inf., Oklahoma, 32d Division, Buna, 26 November 1942.

PVT. GORDON W. EOFF, Inf., Arkansas, 32d Division, Buna, 25 December 1942.

PVT. BERNADINO Y. ESTRADA,* Inf., Arizona, 32d Division, Buna, 16 December 1942.

SGT. WILLIAM F. FALE,* Inf., Wisconsin, 32d Division, Buna, 25 December 1942.

PFC. ALBERT L. FISHER, Inf., Indiana, 32d Division, Buna, 24 December 1942.

SGT. CHESTER C. FUNK, Inf., Washington, 32d Division, Sanananda, 23–24 December 1942.

PVT. HAROLD E. GRABER,* Inf., Tennessee, 32d Division, GHQ, SWPA, 5 December 1942.

TEC. 5 CHARLES H. GRAY, CE, Massachusetts, 32d Division, Buna, 28 December 1942.

PVT. ELMER R. HANGARTNER, Inf., Wisconsin, 32d Division, Buna, 28 December 1942.

Pvt. Earl W. Johnson,* Inf., Ohio, 32d Division, Buna, 23–31 December 1942.

Pvt. Maro P. Johnson, QMC, Illinois, 107th Quartermaster Battalion, Cape Sudest, 16 November 1942.

Pvt. Raymond R. Judd, Inf., Ohio, 32d Division, Tarakena, 12 January 1943.

Sgt. Boyd L. Lincoln,* Inf., Michigan, 32d Division, GHQ, SWPA, 30 November 1942.

S/Sgt. John R. MacGowan, Inf., Wisconsin, 32d Division, GHQ, SWPA, 16 November 1942.

Pvt. Homer W. McAllister, QMC, South Carolina, 107th Quartermaster Battalion, Cape Sudest, 16 November 1942.

Tec. 5 Bart T. McDonough, CE, Massachusetts, 114th Engineer Battalion, Buna, 28 December 1942.

Sgt. Robert R. McGee, Inf., Michigan, 32d Division, Sanananda, 23–28 November 1942.

Pvt. Lawrence B. Marion, Inf., Michigan, 32d Division, Hq. USAFFE, 24 December 1942.

Pvt. Arthur Melanson, CE, Massachusetts, 32d Division, Buna, 28 December 1942.

Pfc. Raymond Milby, Inf., Kentucky, 32d Division, Tarakena, 12 January 1943.

S/Sgt. Milan J. Miljatovich, Inf., Wisconsin, 32d Division, Buna, 28 December 1942.

Cpl. Harold L. Mitchell, Inf., Michigan, 32d Division, Buna, 7–9 December 1942.

Pvt. Earl Mittleberger,* Inf., Iowa, 32d Division, Buna, 28 December 1942.

S/Sgt. John L. Mohl, Inf., Montana, 41st Division, Sanananda, 19 January 1943.

Pvt. Cloyd G. Myers, Inf., Nebraska, 32d Division, Cape Sudest, 16 November 1942.

Pvt. Steve W. Parks, Inf., Wisconsin, 32d Division, Buna, 20 December 1942.

Pvt. Harold O. Pederson, Inf., Ohio, 32d Division, Sanananda, 24 December 1942.

Pvt. Marvin M. Peterson, Inf., Wisconsin, 32d Division, Tarakena, 12 January 1943.

Pfc. Donald R. Price, QMC, Wisconsin, 107th Quartermaster Battalion, Cape Sudest, 16 November 1942.

S/Sgt. John F. Rehak, Jr.,* Inf., Wisconsin, 32d Division, Buna, 20 December 1942.

Cpl. Daniel F. Rini,* Inf., Ohio, 32d Division, Buna, 16 December 1942.

Pfc. Edward R. Rossman, Inf., Indiana, 32d Division, Sanananda, 24 December 1942.

Cpl. Wilmer H. Rummel, Inf., Kansas, 41st Division, Sanananda, 19 January 1943.

S/Sgt. Herman T. Shaw,* Inf., Texas, 32d Division, Buna, 25 December 1942—9 January 1943.

Cpl. Gordon C. Snyder, Inf., Michigan, 32d Division, GHQ, SWPA, 16 November 1942.

Pvt. Lawrence F. Sprague, Inf., Ohio, 32d Division, Tarakena, 12 January 1943.

Pvt. Edward G. Squires, Inf., Ohio, 32d Division, Buna, 28 December 1942.

1st Sgt. Reuben J. Steger,* Inf., Wisconsin, 32d Division, GHQ, SWPA, 21 November 1942.

Cpl. Orrin C. Sutton, Inf., Michigan, 32d Division, Sanananda, 24 December 1942.

S/Sgt. Robert Thompson, Inf., New York, 32d Division, Tarakena, 11 January 1943.

Sgt. Francis J. Vondracek, Inf., Wisconsin, 32d Division, Buna, 24 December 1942.

Sgt. Howard J. Weiss, Inf., Wisconsin, 32d Division, GHQ, SWPA, 16 November 1942.

Sgt. Samuel G. Winzenried, Inf., Wisconsin, 32d Division, Buna, 13 December 1942.

S/Sgt. Paul Ziegele, Inf., Montana, 41st Division, Sanananda, 15 January 1943.

Legion of Merit

1st Lt. Glen V. Blakeslee, Inf., Wisconsin, 32d Division, New Guinea, 16 November 1942–12 February 1943.

Capt. Hiram A. Carpenter, Inf., West Virginia, 32d Division, Soputa, 27 November 1942–11 January 1943.

2D Lt. Lyle E. Hershey, FD, Michigan, 32d Division, Port Moresby, 13 November 1942–10 January 1943.

Maj. Weston A. McCormac, FA, Washington, 41st Division, Oro Bay-Gona, 25 January 1943.

Capt. Marlyn E. Mohr, QMC, Wisconsin, 32d Division, Dobodura, 10 December 1942–14 January 1943.

Capt. William L. Morris, CE, Idaho, 41st Division, Oro Bay-Dobodura, 27 January 1943.

Capt. Walter H. Skielvig, FA, California, 41st Division, New Guinea, 3 January 1943.

WOJG Charles A. Borck, USA, Michigan, 32d Division, Port Moresby, 13 November 1942–20 January 1943.

WOJG Oscar V. Donker, USA, Michigan, 32d Division, Buna-Sanananda, 25 December 1942–28 January 1943.

Pvt. William L. Foxx, QMC, North Carolina, 32d Division, Dobodura, 10 December 1942–14 January 1943.

S/Sgt. John A. Harris, CE, Idaho, 41st Division, Sanananda, 3–25 January 1943.

Sgt. Arthur Molyneux, CE, Idaho, 41st Division, New Guinea, 21 January 1943.

S/Sgt. Bernard F. Persells, QMC, Wisconsin, 32d Division, Dobodura, 10 December 1942–14 January 1943.

S/Sgt. Donald R. Reppenhangen, Inf., Michigan, 32d Division, Soputa-Sanananda, 15 October 1942–16 January 1943.

Sgt. Boyd A. Slaughter, Inf., Michigan, 32d Division, Port Moresby, 1 October 1942–23 January 1943.

1st Sgt. Kenneth J. Sprague, Inf., Michigan, 32d Division, Buna, 12 November 1942–19 January 1943.

M/Sgt. Herbert T. Warren, Inf., Montana, 41st Division, Sanananda, 6–31 January 1943.

Silver Star

1st Lt. Richard J. Adler, Inf., Illinois, 32d Division, Buna, 28 December 1942.

1st Lt. James Angus, Jr., Inf., Illinois, 32d Division, Tarakena, 4–5 January 1943

Capt. Byron A. Armstrong, Inf., Montana, 41st Division, Sanananda Point, 21 January 1943.

LT. COL. CHESTER M. BEAVER, GSC, South Dakota, 32d Division, Cape Sudest, 16 November 1942.

CAPT. WILLIAM C. BENSON, Inf., Montana, 41st Division, Soputa, 16 January 1943.

CAPT. EDMUND C. BLOCH, Inf., Wisconsin, 32d Division, Giruwa, 19 January 1943.

LT. COL. RICHARD D. BOEREM, Inf., Michigan, 32d Division, Soputa, 26 November 1942.

MAJ. JOHN T. BOET, MC, Michigan, 32d Division, Buna, 5 December 1942.

MAJ. GEORGE C. BOND, Inf., Michigan, 32d Division, Soputa, 30 November 1942.

CAPT. FRANK A. BRADBURY, Inf., Montana, 41st Division, Soputa, 9 January 1943.

COL. JOSEPH S. BRADLEY, GSC, South Carolina, 32d Division, Buna, 27 December 1942.

CAPT. WILLIAM W. BRAGG, JR., Inf., West Virginia, 32d Division, Buna Mission, 31 December 1942.

1ST LT. NATHAN BROOKS, MC, Michigan, I Corps, Simemi, 7 December 1942.

CAPT. JAMES M. BUCKLAND, Inf., Montana, 41st Division, Soputa, 20 January 1943.

MAJ. CHARLES R. BUXTON, Inf., Oregon, 41st Division, Ambogo River-Moratee River, 29 January 1943.

1ST LT. ZINA R. CARTER, Inf., Florida, 32d Division, Soputa-Sanananda, 14 December 1942.

1ST LT. JAMES T. COKER, Inf., Oklahoma, 32d Division, Buna, 25 December 1942.

CAPT. JEFFERSON R. CRONK, Inf., Wisconsin, 32d Division, Buna Mission, 31 December 1942.

1ST LT. HERMAN E. DANIELS, Inf., Montana, 41st Division, Soputa, 9 January 1943.

LT. COL. CHARLES R. DAWLEY, Inf., Montana, 41st Division, Soputa, 16 January 1943.

MAJ. LEMUEL E. DAY, MC, Illinois, I Corps, Simemi, 7 December 1942.

CAPT. MICHAEL V. DeFINA, CE, Massachusetts, 32d Division, Simemi, 28 November 1942.

2d Lt. Robert A. Dix, Inf., Wisconsin, 32d Division, Buna, 24 December 1942.

Capt. Oliver O. Dixon, Inf., Indiana, 32d Division, Buna, 10 December 1942.

Lt. Col. Kenneth C. Downing, Inf., Washington, 41st Division, Ambogo River-Moratee River, 28–29 January 1943.

Capt. Duncan V. Dupree,* Inf., Washington, 41st Division, Soputa, 21 January 1943.

Capt. William F. Edwards, MC, Indiana, I Corps, Simemi, 7 December 1942.

Capt. Conway L. Ellers, Inf., Montana, 41st Division, Hq USAFFE, 18–19 January 1943.

1st Lt. Francis J. Endl,* Inf., Wisconsin, 32d Division, Buna, 14–17 December 1942.

Lt. Col. Benjamin R. Farrar, Inf., New Jersey, Hq U. S. Forces Buna, Buna Mission, 22–23 December 1942.

2d Lt. Donald W. Feury,* Inf., Michigan, 32d Division, Buna, 20 December 1942.

1st Lt. Harold R. Fisk, Inf., Idaho, 41st Division, Sanananda Point, 8 January 1943.

1st Lt. William H. Flanagan, Inf., Mississippi, 32d Division, Buna Mission, 28 December 1942.

Capt. Rafael R. Gamso, MC, New York, 32d Division, Buna, 29 December 1942.

Capt. Leonard E. Garrett, Inf., Texas, 32d Division, Buna, 28 December 1942.

Lt. Col. Loren L. Gmeiner, Inf., Wisconsin, 32d Division, Buna, 25 December 1942.

Capt. Lincoln B. Grayson, CE, California, 32d Division, Buna, 22 December 1942.

1st Lt. Julius J. Gutow, MC, Michigan, I Corps, Simemi, 7 December 1942.

Capt. Robert M. Hamilton, Inf., Montana, 41st Division, Soputa, 26 January 1943.

Capt. Clifford P. Hannum, Inf., Indiana, 32d Division, Buna, 29 December 1942.

Maj. Parker C. Hardin, MC, Illinois, Hq U. S. Forces Buna, Hariko, 16 November 1942.

Maj. Gen. Edwin F. Harding, USA, Ohio, 32d Division, Hariko, 16 November 1942.

Maj. Charles W. Hash, Inf., Montana, 41st Division, Soputa, 16 January 1943.

Maj. William D. Hawkins, GSC, New York, 32d Division, Buna, 28 December 1942.

Capt. John L. Hoffman, Inf., Montana, 41st Division, Sanananda, 16 January 1943.

Maj. Stanley W. Hollenbeck, MC, Wisconsin, 32d Division, Embogo, 16–17 November 1942.

Capt. Paul G. Hollister, Inf., Washington, 41st Division, Sanananda, 9 January 1943.

Lt. Col. Merle H. Howe, GSC, Michigan, 32d Division, Tarakena, 16 January 1943.

1st Lt. Bernard P. Howes, Inf., Oklahoma, 32d Division, Soputa-Sanananda, 22 November 1942.

Capt. Robert L. Hughes, Inf., Mississippi, 32d Division, Buna Mission, 2 January 1943.

1st Lt. Paul Keene, Jr., Ord., Kentucky, 32d Division, Buna Mission, 27 December 1942.

2d Lt. Alfred Kirchenbauer, Inf., Michigan, Hq U. S. Forces Buna, Siwori Village, 4–5 January 1943.

1st Lt. Anthony W. Kucera, Inf., Illinois, 32d Division, Buna, 18 December 1942.

Capt. Bevin D. Lee, Inf., South Carolina, 32d Division, Sanananda, 22 November 1942.

Capt. John L. Lehigh, Inf., Indiana, 32d Division, Government Gardens, 28 December 1942.

Lt. Col. Harold M. Lindstrom, Inf., Montana, 41st Division, Soputa, 16 January 1943.

Capt. Howard A. McKinney, Inf., Montana, 41st Division, Soputa, 16 January 1943.

2d Lt. Ben G. McKnight,* Inf., North Carolina, 32d Division, Buna, 16 December 1942.

Capt. John M. Mangano, CE, Massachusetts, 32d Division, Buna, 6 December 1942.

Brig. Gen. Clarence A. Martin, GSC, South Carolina, 32d Division, Buna, 2 December 1942.

1st Lt. Paul H. Maurer, DC, Ohio, 32d Division, Hariko, 16 November 1942.

Capt. Alfred E. Meyer, Inf., Wisconsin, 32d Division, Buna, 16 December 1942.

1st Lt. Leonard J. Milcarek, MC, Illinois, 32d Division, Cape Sudest, 16 November 1942.

1st. Lt. Lester T. Mooney, Inf., Oklahoma, 32d Division, Buna, 26 November 1942.

2d Lt. Bill Mullen, Inf., Nebraska, 32d Division, Buna, 25 December 1942.

Capt. James F. Neely, Inf., Montana, 41st Division, Soputa, 14 January 1943.

Capt. Wendall Noall, MC, Utah, 41st Division, Soputa, 8 January 1943.

Capt. Loren E. O'Dell, Inf., Montana, 41st Division, Sanananda, 21 January 1943.

2d Lt. John E. Oleson,* Inf., Oregon, 41st Division, Sanananda Point, 20 January 1943.

1st Lt. John F. O'Sullivan, CE, Massachusetts, 32d Division, Soputa, 4 December 1942.

1st Lt. Charles E. Peterson, Jr., Inf., Montana, 41st Division, Soputa, 22 January 1943.

Capt. George W. Pugsley, MC, Nebraska, 32d Division, Cape Sudest, 16 November 1942.

Lt. Col. Walter R. Rankin, Inf., Montana, 41st Division, Soputa, 16 January 1943.

Capt. Edward L. Reams, Inf., Montana, 41st Division, Soputa, 21 January 1943.

Capt. Harry L. Richardson, Inf., Virginia, 32d Division, Soputa, 5 December 1942.

Capt. Oliver K. Robinson, Inf., Oregon, 41st Division, Soputa, 16 January 1943.

Capt. Albert F. Rogers, MC, Wisconsin, Hq U. S. Forces Buna, Hariko, 16–23 November 1942.

Col. Gordon B. Rogers, GSC, California, I Corps, Buna, 2 December 1942.

Capt. Richardson D. Roys, Inf., Washington, 41st Division, Soputa, 23 January 1943.

CAPT. DONALD F. RUNNOE, Inf., Michigan, 32d Division, Tarakena, 8 January 1943.

CAPT. EDWARD H. SANDELL,* CWS, Illinois, 32d Division, Buna Mission, 30 November 1942.

2D LT. PAUL L. SCHWARTZ, Inf., New York, 32d Division, Buna, 2 December 1942.

MAJ. HERBERT B. SHIELDS, Jr., MC, Oklahoma, 32d Division, Simemi, 7 December 1942.

2D LT. RICHARD S. SLADE, Inf., Idaho, 41st Division, Sanananda, 19 January 1943.

CAPT. HARRY C. SMITH, MC, Washington, 41st Division, Sanananda, 9 January 1943.

LT. COL. HERBERT A. SMITH, Inf., Wisconsin, 32d Division, Buna, 16 December 1942.

2D LT. RAE M. SMITH, Inf., Minnesota, 32d Division, Mundarupi Village, 8 December 1942.

CAPT. HAROLD A. SPAETZ, Inf., Wisconsin, 32d Division, Pongani, 18 October 1942.

CAPT. JOHN SPONENBURGH, Inf., Montana, 41st Division, Sanananda, 16 January 1943.

CAPT. JOSEPH M. STEHLING, Inf., Wisconsin, 32d Division, Buna Mission, 16 December 1942.

CAPT. LLOYD W. TAYLOR, MC, California, I Corps, Simemi, 7 December 1942.

COL. CLARENCE M. TOMLINSON, Inf., Florida, 32d Division, Buna and Giruwa, 6 December 1942.

CAPT. JACK H. VAN DUYN, Inf., Oregon, 41st Division, Soputa, 16 January 1943.

1ST LT. JOHNEY B. WAX, Inf., Louisiana, 32d Division, Soputa, 23 November 1942.

1ST LT. PAUL WHITAKER,* Inf., Mississippi, 32d Division, Buna, 20 December 1942.

MAJ. JOHN B. WHITE, MC, Oregon, 41st Division, Soputa, 16 January 1943.

1ST LT. ROBERT B. WINKLER, Inf., Wisconsin, 32d Division, Cape Sudest, 16 November 1942.

1ST LT. PHILIP S. WINSON, SC, Michigan, 32d Division, Buna, 23 December 1942.

Pfc. Charles E. Agner, MD, Michigan, 32d Division, Buna Mission, 19 December 1942.

Cpl. Ronald L. Albert, CE, Massachusetts, 32d Division, Dobodura, 30 November 1942.

Pvt. Hugo A. Ambrecht, Inf., Iowa, 32d Division, Buna, 1 January 1943.

Pfc. Lionel R. Anderson, MD, Michigan, 32d Division, Buna, 5 December 1942.

Sgt. Hugo J. Arno, Inf., Wisconsin, 32d Division, Buna, 24 December 1942.

Tec. 5 Kenneth E. Arthur, Inf., Montana, 41st Division, Sanananda Point, 22 January 1943.

Pfc. Julius Aschenbrenner, Inf., Michigan, 32d Division, Buna, 21 November 1942.

Cpl. Charles D. Ashcraft,* Inf., Ohio, 41st Division, Soputa, 9 January 1943.

Tec. 4 Donald Atchinson, Inf., Michigan, 32d Division, Buna, 22–26 November 1942.

Pfc. Wilfred D. Baker, MD, Washington, 41st Division, Sanananda Point, 16 January 1943.

Pvt. Mark E. Barnard, Inf., Montana, 41st Division, Kano, 9 January 1943.

Pfc. William J. Barnett, MD, California, 41st Division, Soputa, 5 January 1943.

Pvt. Wilber C. Bauman, Inf., Ohio, 32d Division, Soputa, 22 November 1942.

Tec. 5 James H. Bay, MD, Washington, 41st Division, Sanananda Point, 19 January 1943.

Cpl. Jean F. Behrendt,* Inf., Wisconsin, 32d Division, Tarakena, 11 January 1943.

Sgt. Arthur Belgarde, Inf., Montana, 41st Division, Soputa, 4 January 1943.

Cpl. Otis Belin, Inf., Texas, 41st Division, Soputa, 14 January 1943.

Tec. 5 Glenn P. Bingham, Inf., Michigan, 32d Division, Buna, 10 December 1942.

Tec. 4 Ralph M. Blake, Inf., Wisconsin, 32d Division, Buna, 24 December 1942.

S/Sgt. Norman J. Bland,* Inf., Michigan, 32d Division, Hq. 32d Division, 1 December 1942.

S/Sgt. Rayborn C. Blank, Inf., Wisconsin, 32d Division, Buna, 18 December and 31 December 1942.

Pfc. Francis A. Bocian, Inf., Illinois, 32d Division, Buna and Tarakena, 19 December 1942–11 January 1943.

1st Sgt. James W. Boland,* Inf., Montana, 41st Division, Soputa, 21 January 1943.

Sgt. Erwin A. Boness,* Inf., Wisconsin, 32d Division, Buna, 22 December 1942.

Pfc. James J. Boorman, Inf., Wisconsin, 32d Division, Buna, 5 December 1942.

Cpl. Dale F. Booth, Inf., Wisconsin, 32d Division, Buna, 5 December 1942.

Sgt. Dudley M. Brice, Inf., Wisconsin, 32d Division, Cape Endaiadere, 26 November 1942.

Pvt. William R. Briggs, Inf., Washington, 32d Division, Cape Sudest, 16 November 1942.

Pfc. Mike Brklacich, Inf., California, 41st Division, Soputa, 19 January 1943.

Sgt. James K. Brower, Inf., Michigan, 32d Division, Buna, 30 November 1942.

S/Sgt. Elmer R. Buchanan, Inf., Michigan, 32d Division, Buna, 16 December 1942.

Pfc. Robert S. Buckowing,* Inf., Michigan, 32d Division, GHQ, SWPA, 8 December 1942.

Tec. 5 Albert C. Burghardt, MD, Michigan, 32d Division, Buna, 5 December 1942.

Cpl. James V. Burrows,* Inf., Michigan, 32d Division, Soputa, 30 November 1942.

Pfc. Victor A. Burt,* Inf., Michigan, 32d Division, Buna, 31 December 1942.

Pfc. Walter J. Campbell, MD, Michigan, 32d Division, Sanananda, 6 December 1942.

Sgt. John Carskadon, Inf., Michigan, 32d Division, Buna, 30 November 1942.

Pfc. Lloyd G. Carter, Inf., Wisconsin, 32d Division, Buna, 26 November 1942.

CPL. WRIGHT C. CHAMBLESS, Inf., Arkansas, 32d Division, Buna, 20 December 1942.

PFC. CLYDE J. CHAPMAN, Inf., Tennessee, 32d Division, Buna, 3 December 1942.

S/SGT. WILLIAM F. CHERRY, MD, Ohio, 32d Division, Cape Sudest, 16 November 1942.

PFC. CARL O. CHRISTENSON, MD, Michigan, 32d Division, Buna, 19 December 1942.

PFC. KENNETH B. CLAPP,* Inf., Mississippi, 32d Division, Buna, 8 December 1942.

SGT. BERNARD F. CLARK,* Inf., Michigan, 32d Division, Sanananda-Soputa, 5 December 1942.

S/SGT. MILTON O. CLINE, Inf., Wisconsin, 32d Division, Buna, 26 November–5 December 1942.

PFC. JOHN R. COAN, Inf., Illinois, 32d Division, Buna, 31 December 1942.

PFC. RAYMOND W. COLLINS, Inf., Iowa, 32d Division, Buna, 1 January 1943.

SGT. ELMER D. COON, Inf., Wisconsin, 32d Division, Buna, 25 December 1942.

PFC. WALTER C. COREY, Inf., Iowa, 32d Division, Buna, 1 January 1943.

S/SGT. ROBERT F. DANENBERG,* Inf., Wisconsin, 32d Division, Hq 32d Div., 26 December 1942.

PFC. CLEVIS T. DARNELL, Inf., Texas, 32d Division, Buna, 3 December 1942.

PVT. EZRA DAVIS, MD, Michigan, 32d Division, Soputa, 2 December 1942.

SGT. STANLEY C. DAVISON, Inf., Montana, 41st Division, Soputa, 15 January 1943.

PFC. RAYMOND E. DERRICK, MD, Oregon, 41st Division, Soputa, 16 January 1943.

SGT. SIDNEY DeVRIES,* Inf., Michigan, 32d Division, Soputa, 23 November 1942.

PVT. VERNON E. DIEGEL, MD, Wisconsin, 32d Division, Pongani, 18 October 1942.

PVT. THOMAS E. DOSS, Inf., Michigan, 32d Division, Buna, 20 December 1942.

Sgt. Leo B. Doubek, Inf., Montana, 41st Division, Soputa, 14 January 1943.

Pfc. Wilson E. Du Bois, Inf., Michigan, 41st Division, Kano, 9 January 1943.

Pfc. Lawrence V. Ekdahl, Ord., Texas, 32d Division, Buna Mission, 16 December 1942.

Pfc. James J. Elliot, Inf., Missouri, 32d Division, Buna, 5 December 1942.

Pfc. Charles O. Ely, Inf., West Virginia, 32d Division, Buna Mission, 8 December 1942.

Pvt. Hymie Y. Epstein,* MD, Nebraska, 32d Division, Soputa, 22 November 1942.

Pvt. Ernest D. Erickson, MD, Iowa, 32d Division, Sanananda, 18 November 1942.

Cpl. Bernardo C. Escobar, Inf., California, 41st Division, Cape Killerton, 9 January 1943.

Tec. 4 Wilfred D. Evans, Inf., Wisconsin, 32d Division, Hariko, 23 December 1942.

Pfc. Lester L. Fall, Inf., Michigan, 32d Division, Buna, 1 January 1943.

Pfc. Robert D. Fandrey, Inf., Iowa, 32d Division, Buna, 17 December 1942.

Tec. 3 William C. Featherstone, Inf., Michigan, 32d Division, Buna, 16 November 1942–3 January 1943.

S/Sgt. Robert E. Fiechter, Inf., Wisconsin, 32d Division, Simemi, 18 November 1942.

Cpl. Glenn W. Follett, Inf., Michigan, 32d Division, Buna, 24 December 1942.

Pfc. Edgar J. Fowler, Inf., Wisconsin, 32d Division, Buna, 31 December 1942.

Pvt. Nathan Freeman, MD, New Jersey, 32d Division, Buna, 29 November 1942.

Sgt. Frank G. Freiberg, Inf., Wisconsin, 32d Division, Buna Mission, 2 January 1943.

Pfc. Joseph R. Freiburger, Inf., Michigan, 32d Division, Soputa, 25 November 1942.

Tec. 5 Paul Frohman, Ord., Pennsylvania, 32d Division, Buna Mission, 27 December 1942.

Pvt. Charles C. Fry, Inf., Illinois, 32d Division, Buna, 11 December 1942.

S/Sgt. Steve E. Fuller,* Inf., Michigan, 32d Division, Sanananda Point, 6 December 1942.

Sgt. Owen D. Gaskell,* Inf., Washington, 41st Division, Sanananda, 5 January 1943.

Pfc. Dell E. Gates, Inf., Nebraska, 32d Division, Cape Endaiadere, 18 December 1942.

Pfc. William L. Gauthier, MD, Michigan, 32d Division, Buna, 21 November 1942.

Pfc. Peter Geelhoed,* Inf., Michigan, 32d Division, Buna Mission, 2 January 1943.

Cpl. Leland L. Genthe, Inf., Wisconsin, 32d Division, Buna, 26 November 1942.

S/Sgt. Victor S. Glenn,* Inf., Wisconsin, 32d Division, Hq 32d Div., 18 December 1942.

Pfc. Howard A. Golding, Inf., Ohio, 32d Division, Buna, 27 December 1942.

Pvt. John R. Goodwin,* Inf., Arkansas, 32d Division, Cape Sudest, 16 November 1942.

Cpl. Paul P. Green, Inf., Wisconsin, 32d Division, Buna, 26 November 1942.

Pfc. James J. Greene, Inf., Wisconsin, 32d Division, Buna, 28 December 1942.

Pfc. Casimier Grych, MD, Wisconsin, 32d Division, Buna, 29 December 1942.

Sgt. Irving W. Hall, Inf., Wisconsin, 32d Division, Buna, 21 November 1942.

Cpl. Charles H. Hallock, Jr.,* Inf., Michigan, 32d Division, Soputa, 2 December 1942.

Cpl. Oscar L. Hanson, Inf., Wisconsin, 32d Division, Cape Sudest, 16 November 1942.

S/Sgt. Alfred C. Hardrath, Inf., Wisconsin, 32d Division, Tarakena, 10 January 1943.

Cpl. Ralph C. Harrison, Inf., Wisconsin, 32d Division, Buna, 21 November 1942.

Tec. 4 Leonard M. Hart, MD, Illinois, 32d Division, Cape Sudest, 16 November 1942.

Pvt. Andrew J. Heck, MD, Michigan, 32d Division, Dobodura, 28 December 1942.

Sgt. George A. Heck, Inf., Indiana, 32d Division, Tarakena, 8 January 1943.

WOJG Daniel J. Herr, USA., New York, 32d Division, Cape Sudest, 16 November 1942.

Cpl. Malcolm H. Hillard, Inf., Michigan, 32d Division, Buna, 20 December 1942.

Sgt. Llewellyn Hoffman, MD, Illinois, 32d Division, Cape Sudest, 16 November 1942.

Pfc. Merl W. Holm,* Inf., Iowa, 32d Division, Sanananda, 26 November 1942.

S/Sgt. Carlton H. Huebner, Inf., Wisconsin, 32d Division, Buna, 24 December 1942.

Pfc. Harold J. Huebner,* MD, Wisconsin, 32d Division, Buna, 20 December 1942.

S/Sgt. Donald F. Hulin, Inf., Washington, 41st Division, Soputa, 20 January 1943.

S/Sgt. Maurice E. Hundahl, Inf., Montana, 41st Division, Sanananda, 19 January 1943.

S/Sgt. Russell C. Huntington, Inf., Michigan, 32d Division, Buna, 28 December 1942.

Pvt. Ray Jackson, MD, Washington, 32d Division, Buna, 29 December 1942.

Cpl. William J. Jacobs, Inf., Michigan, 32d Division, Buna, 8 December 1942.

S/Sgt. Hans M. Jensen, Inf., Wisconsin, 32d Division, Buna, 15 December 1942.

Pvt. Leroy Johnson, Inf., Louisiana, 32d Division, Sanananda, 22 December 1942.

Tec. 5 John Jubera, Jr., MD, Ohio, 32d Division, Buna, 21 November 1942.

Pvt. Donald Kelm, Inf., Illinois, 32d Division, Buna, 28 December 1942.

Pfc. James W. Kice, Inf., Missouri, Hq U. S. Forces Buna, Buna, 21 November 1942.

Sgt. James Kincaid, Inf., California, 32d Division, Hq U. S. Forces Buna, 21 November 1942.

Tec. 5 Francis D. Klein, Inf., Wisconsin, Hq U. S. Forces Buna, Buna, 26 November 1942.

Tec. 5 Max G. Knowles, Inf., Wisconsin, 32d Division, Buna, 28 December 1942.

Pvt. William M. Kurgan, Inf., Illinois, 32d Division, Buna, 15 December 1942.

Sgt. Walter La Faunce,* Inf., Michigan, 32d Division, Sanananda, 26 November 1942.

Pvt. Clare T. Latham,* MD, Michigan, 32d Division, Hq 32d Div., 15 December 1942.

Tec. 4 Irving M. Lawrence, CE, Massachusetts, 32d Division, Buna, 23 December 1942.

Cpl. Rex R. Leland,* Inf., Michigan, 32d Division, Buna, 29 November–5 December 1942.

Pvt. Maurice L. Levy, Inf., Illinois, 41st Division, Sanananda, 19 January 1943.

Pvt. Charles E. Logsdon, Inf., Kentucky, 32d Division, Buna, 28 December 1942.

Pfc. James E. Long, Inf., Michigan, 32d Division, Buna, 26 November 1942.

Tec. 4 James E. Lowthers, Inf., Massachusetts, 32d Division, Buna, 5 December 1942.

Sgt. Einar A. Lund, Inf., Montana, 41st Division, Soputa, 20 January 1943.

Sgt. Murdock E. MacPherson, CE, Massachusetts, 32d Division, Buna, 23 December 1942.

Pfc. Gerald M. McCarthy, MD, Illinois, 32d Division, Buna, 29 December 1942.

Tec. 4 Homer D. McGettigan, Inf., Wisconsin, 32d Division, Simemi, 18 November 1942.

S/Sgt. Frank F. McGuinness, Inf., Montana, 41st Division, Sanananda, 8 January 1943.

Sgt. Lawrence W. McNight, Inf., Nevada, 41st Division, Sanananda, 8 January 1943.

Pvt. John I. Manning, Inf., Michigan, 32d Division, Hq U. S. Forces Buna, 21 November 1942.

T/Sgt. Edgar C. Marsh, Inf., Michigan, 32d Division, Buna, 3 December 1942.

Pfc. Harold L. Marshall, MD, Kentucky, 41st Division, Soputa, 9 January 1943.

Pfc. Gerald Massey, Inf., Indiana, 32d Division, Sanananda, 22 December 1942.

Sgt. George L. May,* Inf., Michigan, 32d Division, Soputa, 30 November 1942:

Sgt. Charles I. Maynor, Inf., Wisconsin, 32d Division, Buna Mission, 24 December 1942.

Pvt. Emil G. Medvin, Inf., Ohio, 32d Division, Hq. U. S. Forces Buna, 21 November 1942.

Sgt. Aaron Meyers, Inf., Missouri, 32d Division, Buna, 15 December 1942.

Pvt. George K. Miller, Inf., Missouri, 32d Division, Hq. U. S. Forces Buna, 23 December 1942.

Sgt. Donald J. Milton, Inf., Wisconsin, 32d Division, Government Gardens, 24 December 1942.

Pfc. Edward A. Modrzejewski, Inf., Michigan, 32d Division, Buna, 30 November 1942.

Pfc. Jack C. Moore, MD, Wyoming, 32d Division, Giruwa, 19 January 1943.

Sgt. Ralph S. Morris, Inf., Washington, 41st Division, Sanananda, 22 January 1943.

Cpl. Donald R. Muench, Inf., Wisconsin, 32d Division, Buna, 26 November 1942.

Sgt. Ralph W. Nay, Inf., Montana, 41st Division, Sanananda Point, 7 January 1943.

Sgt. Emil L. Nelson, Inf., Montana, 41st Division, Sanananda Point, 8 January 1943.

Pvt. O'Donnell O'Brien, Inf., Michigan, 32d Division, Buna, 30 November 1942.

Pvt. Louis Ochoa, Inf., Arizona, 32d Division, Buna, 24 December 1942.

S/Sgt. Kenneth V. Olberg, Inf., Montana, 41st Division, Soputa, 19 January 1943.

Sgt. Willard L. Oles, Inf., Michigan, 32d Division, Soputa, 26 November–13 December 1942.

Pfc. William H. Oliver, Inf., Arizona, 32d Division, Buna, 30 November 1942.

Sgt. Victor L. Olson, Inf., Wisconsin, 32d Division, Buna, 5 December 1942.

Sgt. Ralph W. Oswald, Inf., Montana, 41st Division, Sanananda Point, 19 January 1943.

Pvt. Robert J. Packard,* Inf., Wisconsin, 32d Division, Buna, 15 December 1942.

Sgt. Carl J. Patrinos, Inf., Wisconsin, 32d Division, Giruwa, 17 January 1943.

Pfc. Paul T. Phillips, Ord., Michigan, 32d Division, Buna Mission, 16 December 1942.

Cpl. Richard J. Pieh, Inf., Michigan, 32d Division, Buna, 16 December 1942.

S/Sgt. Louis H. Pollister, CE, Massachusetts, 32d Division, Buna, 28 December 1942.

Pvt. John J. Potts,* Inf., Illinois, 41st Division, Sanananda, 14 January 1943.

S/Sgt. Harold E. Poynter, Inf., Montana, 41st Division, Sanananda, 9 January 1943.

1st Sgt. George Pravda, Inf., Michigan, 32d Division, Buna Mission, 30 November 1942.

Pfc. Rex N. Purk, MD, Michigan 32d Division, Buna, 25 December 1942.

Sgt. Howard C. Purtyman, Inf., Arizona, 32d Division, Hq U. S. Forces Buna, 16 December 1942.

Pvt. Vernon H. Pyles, MD, Kentucky, 32d Division, Buna, 29 December 1942.

Pfc. Joe H. Rainwater,* Inf., Texas, 32d Division, Buna Mission, 4 January 1943.

S/Sgt. Emil Raninen, Ord., Michigan, 32d Division, Government Gardens, 30 December 1942.

Cpl. George D. Rawson,* Inf., Wisconsin, 32d Division, Buna Mission, 31 December 1942.

S/Sgt. Donald N. Rea,* Inf., Michigan, 32d Division, Hq 32d Div., 26 November 1942.

S/Sgt. Joseph Reddoor, Inf., Montana, 41st Division, Soputa, 4 January 1943.

Cpl. Frank H. Reese, Inf., Wisconsin, 32d Division, Simemi, 18 November 1942.

SGT. VICTOR J. REIGEL, Inf., Wisconsin, 32d Division, Buna, 19 November 1942.

PVT. EDWARD L. REISING, MD, Ohio, 32d Division, Pongani, 17 November 1942.

PVT. BENNIE B. RICHELL, Inf., Illinois, 32d Division, Buna, 30 November 1942.

PFC. CLYDE RIDGE, Inf., Oklahoma, 32d Division, Buna, 31 December 1942.

PVT. ROBERT RIEF, Inf., Michigan, 32d Division, Soputa-Sanananda, 6 December 1942.

PVT. DOUGLAS C. ROGERS, Inf., Michigan, 32d Division, Hq U. S. Forces Buna, 20 December 1942.

PFC. SHELBY M. ROOF, Inf., Nebraska, 32d Division, Pongani, 18 October 1942.

CPL. LAWRENCE A. ROWE, Inf., Indiana, 32d Division, Buna, 23 November 1942.

PVT. ALBERT L. RUSSELL, Jr.,* CE, Pennsylvania, 32d Division, Hq 32d Div., 6 December 1942.

CPL. ALONZO RUSSELL, Inf., Wisconsin, 32d Division, Buna, 28 December 1942.

PVT. SAM J. SCARFO, MD, Ohio, 32d Division, Buna, 29 December 1942.

PFC. AARON A. SCHABO,* Inf., Wisconsin, 32d Division, Buna, 4 January 1943.

PVT. ROBBIE H. SCHEEF, Inf., Nebraska, 32d Division, Soputa, 2 December 1942.

SGT. ERNEST R. SEARFOSS, Inf., Michigan, 32d Division, Government Gardens, 1 January 1943.

SGT. LELAND L. SHARP,* Inf., Michigan, 32d Division, Buna Mission, 27 December 1942.

PVT. ROBERT M. SHEARER, Inf., Mississippi, 32d Division, Soputa, 2 December 1942.

S/SGT. RUSSELL E. SIGWELL, Inf., Wisconsin, 32d Division, Buna, 18 November 1942.

SGT. ROBERT H. SIMMONS, Inf., Wisconsin, 32d Division, Government Gardens, 25 December 1942.

SGT. ALBIN C. SIPE, Jr., Inf., Washington, 41st Division, Sanananda Point, 22 January 1943.

PFC. KARL SKYEE, Inf., Michigan, 32d Division, Soputa, 2 December 1942.

SGT. HERBERT E. SMITH,* Inf., Wisconsin, 32d Division, Buna, 21 November 1942.

TEC. 5 ROBERT L. SMITH, Inf., California, 32d Division, Cape Sudest, 16 November 1942.

PVT. JESSE S. SOMMER,* Inf., Illinois, 32d Division, Sanananda, 5 December 1942.

PFC. ROBERT F. STRONG, Inf., Michigan, 32 Division, Buna Mission, 30 November 1942.

PFC. FLOYD A. SUJKOWSKI, Inf., Michigan, 32d Division, Hq U. S. Forces, Buna, 20 December 1942.

CPL. MATTHEW SUSJLE, Inf., Illinois, 32d Division, Buna, 26 November 1942.

CPL. ROBERT J. TAPPEN, Inf., Michigan, 32d Division, Buna, 19 November 1942.

CPL. MERLE G. TASKER,* Inf., Michigan, 32d Division, Government Gardens, 1 January 1943.

SGT. WILLIAM B. TAYLOR,* Inf., Oregon, 41st Division, Soputa, 23 January 1943.

CPL. WILBUR G. TIRRELL, CE, Massachusetts, 32d Division, Buna, 8 December 1942.

SGT. CARL R. TRAUB, Inf., Wisconsin, 32d Division, Buna, 1 January 1943.

S/SGT. HARRY C. TRODICK, Inf., Montana, 41st Division, Sanananda, 20 January 1943.

SGT. WILLIAM C. TULLIS, Inf., Michigan, 32d Division, Sanananda, 9 January 1943.

TEC. 5 WALLACE I. VANCOR, CE, Massachusetts, 32d Division, Buna, 23 December 1942.

S/SGT. HARRY J. VAN DE RIET, Inf., Montana, 41st Division, Soputa, 19 January 1943.

PFC. WILLIAM E. VIDER,* MD, Minnesota, 32d Division, Buna, 5 December 1942.

CWO HUGO H. VOELKLI, USA, Wisconsin, 32d Division, Cape Sudest, 16 November 1942.

S/SGT. CHARLES E. WAGNER, Inf., Wisconsin, 32d Division, Buna, 28 December 1942.

Pfc. Edward W. Walters,* Inf., Colorado, 32d Division, Buna, 1 January 1943.

Pvt. Ernest J. Weber, Inf., Wisconsin, 32d Division, Buna, 5 December 1942.

Pfc. Harold J. Wells, MD, Saskatchewan, Canada, 32d Division, Cape Sudest, 16 November 1942.

Sgt. James P. Welsh,* Inf., Wisconsin, 32d Division, Buna, 21 November 1942.

1st Sgt. Alfred R. Wentzloff, Inf., Michigan, 32d Division, Sanananda, 1 December 1942.

Pfc. Theodore I. Wiercinski, Inf., Michigan, 32d Division, Hariko, 18 November 1942.

Pvt. Jack M. Williams,* Inf., Alabama, 32d Division, Buna Mission, 1 January 1943.

Pvt. Dale F. Wimer, Inf., Wisconsin, 32d Division, Buna, 20 November 1942.

S/Sgt. Ivan J. Yearman, Inf., Wisconsin, 32d Division, Buna, 21 November 1942.

S/Sgt. Russell E. Young, Inf., Michigan, 32d Division, Soputa, 2 December 1942.

Sgt. Paul Ziegele, Inf., Montana, 41st Division, Sanananda, 15 January 1943.

Oak Leaf Cluster

Capt. William C. Benson, Inf., Montana, 41st Division, Soputa, 9 January 1943, Oak Leaf Cluster to Silver Star.

Capt. Edmund C. Bloch, Inf., Wisconsin, 32d Division, Tarakena, 5–8 January 1943, Oak Leaf Cluster to Silver Star.

Capt. Herman J. F. Bottcher, Inf., California, 32d Division, Buna, 20 December 1942, Oak Leaf Cluster to Distinguished Service Cross.

Col. Joseph S. Bradley, GSC, South Carolina, 32d Division, Hq. U. S. Forces Buna, 11 January 1943, Oak Leaf Cluster to Silver Star.

Col. John J. Carew, CE, Massachusetts, 32d Division, Buna, 23 December 1942, Oak Leaf Cluster to Silver Star.

Col. John E. Grose, Inf., West Virginia, I Corps, Buna, 5 December 1942, Oak Leaf Cluster to Silver Star.

2D Lt. Bill Mullen, Inf., Nebraska, 32d Division, Hq. 32 Div., 25 December 1942, Oak Leaf Cluster to Silver Star.

1st Lt. Herbert G. Peabody, Inf., Vermont, 32d Division, Buna, 5 December 1942, Oak Leaf Cluster to Distinguished Service Cross.

Col. Clarence M. Tomlinson, Inf., Florida, 32d Division, Soputa, 26 December 1942, Oak Leaf Cluster to Silver Star.

1st Sgt. George Pravda, Inf., Michigan, 32d Division, Buna, 1 December 1942, Oak Leaf Cluster to Silver Star.

Pfc. Rex N. Purk, MD, Michigan, 32d Division, Buna, 20 December 1942, Oak Leaf Cluster to Silver Star.

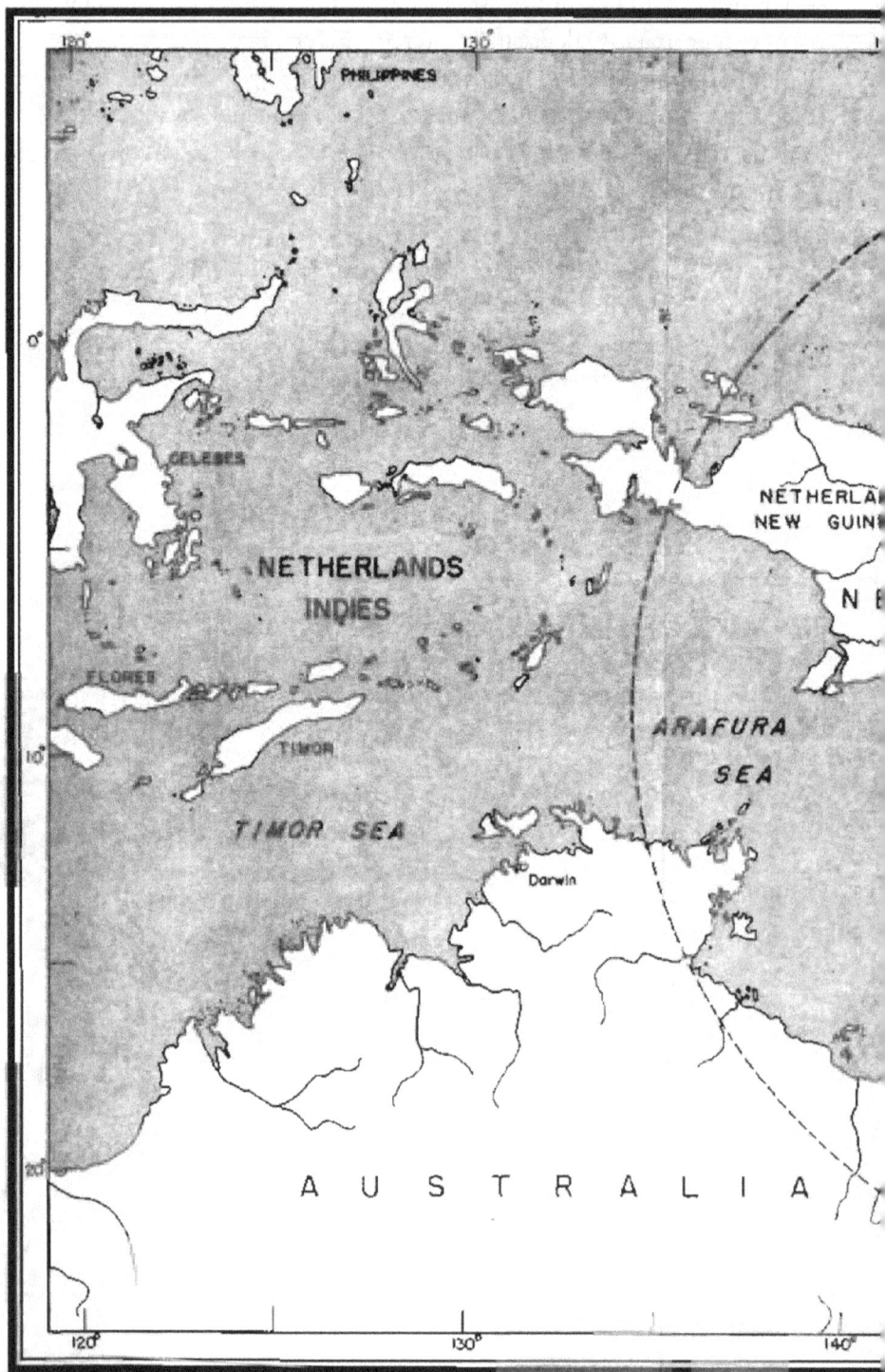

RELATION OF NEW GUINEA
TO NEIGHBORING AREA

SCALE

100   0   100   200   300   400   500   600 miles

SINUSOIDAL EQUAL-AREA PROJECTION

Cartographic Section, Diss Unit by J R.Hagan

387792 O – 44   Inside back cover

www.ingramcontent.com/pod-product-compliance
Lightning Source LLC
Chambersburg PA
CBHW060543100426
42742CB00013B/2435